Scheduling
and Teaching
Music

Larry R. Blocher
Richard B. Miles

Table of Contents

Chapter 4: **Descriptions of School Music Programs** *continued*

Acknowledgments

The authors gratefully acknowledge the many music educators, administrators, students, and colleagues who have shared information concerning the issues addressed in our book. We would like to thank the *National Association of School Music Dealers* (NASMD) for caring enough about the music teachers, music students, and music programs in this country to provide partial funding for this project. These important folks understand, individually and collectively, that music education does indeed matter. Special thanks to Denny Senseney, President of Senseney Music in Wichita, Kansas, for his leadership, support, and friendship.

We thank the office staff of the Morehead State University Bands, especially Tammy Bradley, former secretary, and the many undergraduate and graduate students of Morehead and Wichita State who assisted with the numerous research projects. A special note of thanks goes to the *Morehead State University Department of Music and University Bands* and to the *Wichita State University School of Music* for supporting our interest in providing this information.

We also acknowledge the following for their research grants and funding of our state surveys and research projects on school scheduling and the teaching of music:

Kansas Music Educators Association

The Kentucky Coalition for Music Education

Kentucky Music Educators Association – District 8

Indiana Department of Education

Michigan School Band and Orchestra Association

MidWest International Band and Orchestra Board of Directors

Texas Music Educators Association

Wisconsin Music Educators Association

Finally, thanks to the many music education professionals across the country who took the time to assist. They continue to set the pace for all of us.

Foreword

Scheduling and Teaching Music is a much-needed text that addresses the important needs of school music teachers in an ever-changing world of education. The text provides a wealth of information that guides you through the maze and complexities of today's scheduling practices while providing instructional strategies that allow you to *get to the good stuff* that produces music programs of merit.

The text contains examples of teaching and scheduling strategies, scheduling implications for music programs, creating variety in daily rehearsals and performances, using time wisely/time-saving strategies, instructional time, building resources, and lesson planning. These are but a few of the important areas dealing with the real issues of teaching in today's schools. The collections of teaching and scheduling strategies, along with creative ideas for varying daily rehearsals, are invaluable for music educators. As stated by the authors, "It is a book about music teachers who have done and continue to do their homework. It is a book about how these teachers teach music because of, in spite of, and regardless of alternative teaching schedules." This text is a massive contribution to our teaching profession and is essential reading for in-service music teachers, pre-service music teachers, music teachers who teach other music teachers, administrators who work with music teachers and music students, and for anyone interested in teaching music through performance in today's schools.

As state and national efforts alter the "face of education," discussion and diversity continue in a quest to provide solutions for school music programs. This publication effectively fills the gap when dealing with such complexities. The authors have cleared the avenue to *get to the good stuff* and guide you through the ever-changing world of education.

— Edward S. Lisk
Clinician, Conductor, Author

"There is a crisis in American Education. Or maybe there isn't. There used to be. Several actually. But maybe there weren't. Maybe there always is."

— Gregory J. Cizek

Chapter One:

Let's See You Do It!

"A teacher affects eternity; he can
never tell where his influence
stops."

— *Henry Adams*

Scenario

A few years ago, one of our favorite colleagues was serving as a guest conductor of a regional high school honor band. Late in the afternoon of what had been a successful but long rehearsal day, our colleague was rehearsing a section of the music that was proving to be particularly challenging for the trumpets. Finally, following several well-intended, but less than productive, minutes of rehearsing the trumpets repeatedly at letter C, a frustrated voice from the far end of the trumpet section shouted, **"Let's see you do it!"** Our colleague moved on to letter D.

Getting to the Good Stuff

Let's see you do it! Every day, music teachers at all levels, in a variety of teaching situations, accept the challenge to do *it* — just do it — just teach music. Just teach music. It's what music teachers do. A few years ago, we attended a clinic session at the MidWest International Band and Orchestra Conference presented by Bob Duke from the University of Texas at Austin. Bob was outlining strategies that music teachers could use to help children become more engaged in the music learning process. Now while Bob was quick to point out there were no *quick fixes* in dealing with real children, he did suggest that, regardless of the teaching situation, teachers needed to provide opportunities for students to get to the *good stuff* in music as quickly as possible. As ensemble directors — music teachers who teach music through performance in choir, band, and/or orchestra — we get to decide not only what the good stuff is in music, but also how to help our students get to the good stuff in our individual music teaching situations.

Making Decisions

For a long time now, we have believed that teachers are decision makers. Actually, the *teacher as decision maker* was a phrase we memorized as young college teachers because it was part of a College of Education mission statement that all education faculty (music education, too) were expected to know as a part of an NCATE visitation. Once NCATE was a fond memory, we decided we liked the idea of being decision makers. Decision making in music teaching starts early in one's career, continues for a teaching lifetime, and, when applied to music instruction, involves thinking about some *big ideas:* what to teach, how to teach, how to know whether students got the *it* that you were trying to teach, and, perhaps most importantly, deciding why anyone should know or be able to do what you wanted them to know or be able to do in the first place.

Philosophy Re-visited

This *why* idea seems to border dangerously close to the need for a philosophy of music teaching. While thinking about music teaching philosophy may bring back memories of educational *hoop jumping,* key questions seem to underlie our educational decision making as music teachers: What is it that we want our students to learn and remember from their rehearsal and performance experiences in orchestra, choir, and/or band? Or, put another way, how can we teach our students about music through performance so that music will have a chance to be an important, ongoing part of their lives for a lifetime?

One Size Does Not Fit All

There are probably no quick-fix, all-purpose, universal answers to these questions. Every music teaching situation is unique. However, teaching for the development of student performance skills while teaching for musical understanding — getting to the good stuff in music teaching — staying focused on what is *best* for all students — does require desire and planning by **all** music teachers. And since we appear to be living at a time when, at least in education, one of the only constants seems to be change, music teachers, as a part of this planning, must also be willing to do their professional *homework* in order to have the *best* information when making decisions about the many *new* ideas brought about by the current school reform movement. What has been called an alternative scheduling movement, a kind of movement within a movement (don't you just love education?), has been described as a catalyst for change in high schools. According to recent estimates, over 50% of secondary schools in the United States are currently using or considering the adoption of some form of alternative scheduling. Informal reports suggest that a growing number of middle schools and elementary schools are also involved with scheduling changes. Additionally, a growing number of music teachers are facing year-round scheduling. There is simply not one way to deal with all of these scheduling scenarios — one size does not fit all.

Why We Wrote This Book

This is a book about scheduling and teaching music. It is written for in-service music teachers, pre-service music teachers, music teachers who teach other music teachers, administrators who work with music teachers and music students, and for anyone interested in teaching music through performance in today's schools. It is not a book that champions or bashes any form of scheduling. It is a book about music teachers who have done, and continue to do, their homework. It is a book about what these teachers have learned and continue to learn about teaching music using a variety of schedules. It is a book about how these music teachers teach music because of, in spite of, and/or regardless of alternative teaching schedules. Some of these music teachers have lots of time to teach music and some have enough time to teach music. Others do not. The bottom line: music teachers — band directors, choir directors, and orchestra directors — continue to report that teaching music through performance is still teaching music through performance regardless of the schedule in use. However, longer, shorter, and alternating *blocks* of time are dictating a need for more rehearsal variety, more creative teaching strategies, and/or more efficient use of time in rehearsals. Let's see you do it! — get to the good stuff — our challenge to **just teach music** continues.

Chapter Two

Does Anybody Really Know What Time It Is?

Alternate Use of School Time

Why alternative scheduling and why now? While there is probably not one single answer, the *short version* seems to suggest a collective desire to improve school effectiveness (the reader is encouraged to consult the resources listed at the end of this book for more detailed information). Research conducted on the use of school time over the last several years suggests that the single-period day — in effect in American schools for the past 70 years with one notable departure — is impersonal and unfriendly to both students and teachers, and limiting with regard to instructional and learning possibilities. This research suggests that the single-period day contributes to the ineffective use of instructional time.[1] Public Law 102-62 (The Education Council Act of 1991) established the National Commission on Time and Learning. The Commission's report, *Prisoners of Time,* released in April, 1994, stated that "Time is the missing element in our great national debate about learning and the need for higher standards for all students." The report characterized learning in America as a *prisoner of time,* and called for schools to be reinvented around learning, not time.[2]

Scheduling Reform Goals

In 1995, Canady and Rettig suggested that the criticism surrounding traditional scheduling had "sparked a nation-wide review of high school scheduling practices and a search for models better able to meet the needs of teachers and students."[3] Current goals of the high school scheduling reform movement, according to Canady and Rettig, include creating high school schedules which are designed to:

- Reduce the number of class changes and movements required for large groups of students each day;

- Reduce the duplication and inefficiency reported in many high schools using a daily, single-period schedule;

- Reduce the number of student/teacher contacts and preparations required each day;

- Reduce the fragmentation reported in many single-period classes;

- Provide teachers and students with large blocks of teaching and learning time, encouraging active teacher/student involvement.[4]

With the possible exception of reducing the number of student/teacher contacts each day (we don't know too many music teachers who want fewer students in their ensembles or music programs), the goals provide at least a theoretical basis for understanding why we are where we are with block scheduling today.

Implications for School Music Programs

If you are reading this book looking for **the answer** on how to deal with alternative scheduling, you might be reading the wrong book. There simply is not one way to deal with alternative scheduling. It is important to remember that the effects of school reform — including alternative scheduling — are not uniform. As we work our way through the research and resulting implications of alternative scheduling for school music programs, each reader is encouraged to think about his/her individual school music program, to think about the real students in these programs, and to make application of information that seems to fit individual situations.

The information presented here has been gathered from public school music teachers for music teachers. The objective of our research has never been to present alternative scheduling as good, bad, or ugly (although we have discovered individual music programs whose schedules reportedly fit each description). Our goal continues to be to present what *is* with regard to alternative scheduling according to the experts — public school music teachers across the country.

Initial Reports

For the past few years we have been looking at the impact of block scheduling implementation on performance and non-performance music classes in secondary schools across the country. Our initial work focused in the states of Kentucky, Indiana, Michigan, and Wisconsin. We collected and analyzed data gathered from more than 190 high school music programs in these states during a period between 1994 and 1996. High school music teachers in band, chorus, and orchestra were asked to provide information about the type of block scheduling in use and the length of time the scheduling plan had been in place, specific enrollment trends, scheduling conflicts, and advantages/disadvantages experienced with current block schedules. Our data analyses (based on a 99% director response rate), indicated that, in general, music programs across all school sizes that were utilizing some form of a modified block schedule reported less difficulty with enrollment problems and scheduling conflicts than music programs in schools using a 4x4 block schedule. Additionally, school schedules designed to fit individual school needs seemed to provide the *best* initial results. School administrator support was considered important to music program success. While these data may be important in understanding the impact of block scheduling on the particular schools that were part of these studies, care should be taken when generalizing these results to other school situations.

Ten Important Ideas

The next step in our research involved gathering information from school music teachers from around the country who reported that block scheduling seemed to be working. The focus here was to look at the process that these music teachers were using to structure their program's success, and to identify scheduling models that might be used as starting places for music teachers in similar situations. Once again music teachers reported a need to work with school colleagues for success. Scheduling models identified were designed to *fit* specific school needs (detailed results may be found in *Block Scheduling: Implications for Music Education*).

It is important to note, as previously stated, that the results of the empirical studies that we are aware of (our own included), are based on information provided by music teachers. Many times these teachers indicated that, at the time, they had been working with a particular block scheduling design for a relatively short period of time (one to two years in many cases). Time may be an important factor.

What are the implications for block scheduling on school music programs? Each situation may, indeed, be different. However, music teachers have reported varying levels of success/concern in dealing with block scheduling in the following areas:

1. Maintaining student enrollment in school music programs.

2. Scheduling conflicts with AP classes and electives.

3. Maintaining ensemble balance.

4. Students able to enroll in more than one music class at one time.

5. Offering anything other than performance classes.

6. Time for reinforcement.

7. Dealing with school days that are *missed*.

8. Schedules for *traveling* music teachers (from building to building and/or level to level).

9. The performance level of music students.

10. Dealing with altered (longer, shorter, and alternating) blocks of teaching time.

Teaching Time

Number 10 from the previous list — dealing with altered blocks of teaching time — appears to be an important issue for many music teachers, according to one of our most recent studies completed during the 1997-98 school year. The project, funded by the National Association of School Music Dealers (NASMD), involved more than 200 secondary music programs nationally, and attempted to identify strategies currently used by successful music teachers to keep students *engaged* (jargon is a wonderful thing, isn't it?) and learning both the music and about music during these altered blocks of teaching/learning time. Music teachers in band, chorus, and orchestra reported that while the big objectives for teaching music through performance remained the same regardless of the schedule in use, new time parameters were presenting new challenges for them in dealing with student fatigue and concentration, and rehearsal pacing and organization. Many of these music teachers were challenged to re-think their teaching strategies in order to add rehearsal variety and make more efficient use of rehearsal time in order to structure student musical success. As one director stated: "We felt that our students would not be able to play or sing for 90 minutes. We had to find another way to deal with this amount of time." Music teachers in this performance-based program broke down the block and included a more comprehensive music approach that is reportedly meeting not only the performance goals of the program, but also providing a more comprehensive music education for their students (detailed suggestions from public school music teachers for creating rehearsal variety, using creative teaching strategies, and using time efficiently may be found in the following chapters).

Suggestions

Music teachers from around the country have offered a variety of suggestions for music teachers working with alternative scheduling. The number one suggestion has been to *become or stay informed*. Additionally, music teachers have challenged other music teachers to have the facts and to do their homework (the resource section of this book may help in this area). Other common suggestions have included:

- Get in on the ground floor — get on the scheduling committee

- Build coalitions with other curricular areas

- Establish early and frequent communication with your administration

- Be a team player

- Keep the focus on what is best for the students' education[5]

Kevin Meidl from Appleton West High School in Wisconsin offers the following suggestions for what music teachers should not do:

> "Be careful to be a problem solver, and not just an obstacle for the block scheduling committee to overcome. Parent groups can be helpful, but don't enlist the army unless you have thought well about the consequences. It is easy with this issue to appear self-serving and not open to other educational needs of the student."[6]

Ideas to Consider

Doug Bakkum from Blaine High School in Minnesota offers the following ideas for music teachers to consider:

1. Why is your building looking towards change?
   - to eliminate teachers
   - to create more options for teachers
   - change for change's sake
   - reduce frantic pace of day (it will)

2. How will this impact staffing?
   - can you justify a student/teacher ratio equal to non-music teachers

3. Every day? All year? Eight-five minutes?

4. Impact on music budgets?
   - more time means more repair
   - more time means more literature
   - more time means more copy budget (theory, rhythm, ear training, listening assignments)

5. Can students be in more than one group?
   - Band and Choir
   - Band or Orchestra *and* Choir

6. Impact on non-performance music classes?
   - can you require enrollment in one music class concurrently with another

7. How many single section, non-music courses that would conflict with a music course will be offered?

8. Private lesson programs?
   - during the day
   - after school

9. Team teaching? (instead of lesson pull-out program)

10. Marching Band — Pep Band?
    - class band required
    - during school day
    - additional staffing
    - for credit

11. Jazz ensemble?
    - class band required

- during school day
- for credit

12. Technology implementation?
    - we use Vivace and other software

13. Will other *required* courses meet more than two quarters?
    - our social studies AP courses do — we are large enough so this doesn't seem to be hurting us

14. Will kids be required to commit for the entire year?
    - ours are required

15. Do you have a strong AP program — those *perceived required* classes?

16. Is building staff driven by student registration?
    - our students register in February
    - computer system schedules with over 94% accuracy (the first run)
    - our staffing is done based on registration

17. Will your facility handle the shift?
    - each room now offers only four teaching stations per day (instead of seven)

18. Does your principal trust your word?

19. Do you trust your administration's word?

20. What are you doing to build trust?

21. Are you building effective communication between staff, administration, and supervisors?
    - are you allowing others to help you?
    - do you keep your supervisor/curriculum people informed?

22. Can students request specific teachers when they register?
    - some schools allow this — this may further compound scheduling problems

23. What are you doing to create an awareness of the HS program in the middle school?
    - can you recruit?
    - work to integrate curriculum vertically 5-12

24. How strongly does your faculty value your music program?
    - when push comes to shove, will they support you?
    - can you hold your own in turf discussions without losing your cool?

25. What is the single most important aspect of your music program?
    - determine your best case, worst case — be willing to listen
    - prioritize everything
    - you will be asked to offer compromise, be ready with options

26. What can you offer as a compromise to reach your department goals?

27. Are you willing to completely re-design your approach to instruction?

28. Can you justify every dollar that you currently spend as essential to curriculum needs?
    - when staffing shifts occur, budgets will soon follow — be ready to justify more funding

29. Can you discuss problems and solutions effectively and calmly?
    - do you have your administration's ear?
    - can your music supervisor assist you?

30. Separate emotional fears and responses from reactions and discussion
    - plan! plan! plan!

31. Listen to the questions other staff are asking administration regarding the switch
    - this will tell you their fears, turf issues, priorities
    - use this information in your relationship building — become a good listener

32. Is this best for students in your school?
    - does anybody ask?
    - is there solid data to justify a change? (I still can't find valid data)

33. Is this best for your community?
    - are parents involved?

Doug continues: "As I visit programs around the country, the one factor that seems to be consistent is that schools that are willing to personalize their programs to meet the needs of their students tend to do the best. What works for one may not work for anyone else. There are just too many variables between schools. Relationships and trust are huge factors. Administrators and music directors must have a level of trust regarding change and progress. Music programs without support from administrators, staff, parents, and students will die quickly under any circumstance. Music teachers must re-evaluate and decide what is truly most important and must be maintained during any kind of change. Working from this core value may help answer future questions regarding implementation. There is no quick fix — no 'try before you buy.' The circumstances of each school will dictate what direction should be taken."[7]

Where We Are

The *jury is still out* remains the best description of the effects of block scheduling on school music programs at this time. Canady and Rettig suggest that the implementation of a new schedule is not an end in itself. What we do as music teachers to, for, and with our music students in our music classrooms (rehearsals), continues to be the most critical component of any change effort.

Endnotes

[1]Robert Canady and Michael Rettig, *Block Scheduling: A Catalyst for Change in High Schools* (Princeton, NJ: Eye On Education, 1995), pp. 3-11.

[2]National Education Commission on Time and Learning, *Prisoners of Time,* 1994, p. 7.

[3]Canady and Rettig, *Block Scheduling: A Catalyst for Change in High Schools,* p. 12.

[4]Ibid.

[5]Richard Miles and Larry Blocher, *Block Scheduling: Implications for Music Education* (Springfield, IL: Focus On Excellence, 1996), pp. 179-181.

[6]Kevin Meidl, "Block Scheduling and the Performance Based Music Program," paper presented at the biennial meeting of the Music Educators National Conference, Phoenix, AZ, 1998.

[7]Doug Bakkum, "Block Scheduling: Issues You Must Consider When Faced With the Implementation of the 4 Period Day," paper presented at the biennial meeting of the Music Educators National Conference, Phoenix, AZ, 1998.

Chapter Three

Remember
The Bird Seed

Scenario

A man walked into a pet store to buy a bird that would talk. The pet store owner told the man that he had the perfect bird to fit his request, the purchase was made, and the man headed home with the bird. The next day the man returned to the pet store and complained to the pet store owner that the bird would not talk. The pet store owner asked the man if he had purchased a little bell for the bird to peck, because the bird simply would not talk until he had pecked on his little bell. The man purchased the bell. The next day the man returned to the pet store and once again complained to the pet store owner that the bird would not talk. The pet store owner asked the man if he had purchased a little ladder for the bird to climb, because the bird simply would not talk until he had pecked on his little bell and climbed up his little ladder. The man purchased the ladder. The next day the man returned to the pet store and once again complained to the pet store owner that the bird would still not talk. The pet store owner asked the man if he had purchased a little mirror for the bird, because the bird simply would not talk until he had pecked on his little bell, climbed up his little ladder, and looked in his little mirror. The man purchased the little mirror. The next day the man returned to the pet store and once again complained to the pet store owner that the bird would not talk. The pet store owner asked the man if he had purchased a little swing for the bird because he simply would not talk until he had pecked on his little bell, climbed up his little ladder, looked in his little mirror, and jumped on his little swing. The man purchased the little swing. The next day the man returned to the pet store and told the pet store owner that his bird was dead. The pet store owner, shaking his head in disbelief, asked how such a thing could have happened. The man replied that he had watched that morning while the bird pecked on his little bell, climbed up his little ladder, looked in his little mirror, jumped on his little swing, looked him in the eye and said; "Mister, you forgot to buy bird seed."

It is easy for us as music teachers to get so caught up in the bells, ladders, mirrors, and swings of our music teaching environment (4 x 4 schedules, modified schedules, alternating day schedules... you get the idea), that it is sometimes difficult to remain focused on both the bird and the bird seed — our students, the music that we choose to rehearse and perform, and our plan for teaching the music.

Music Teachers and Music Students

Bob Spradling, Director of Bands at Western Michigan University, once said that only two things really matter in education — teachers and students. In what he has called a **motivational interaction sequence**, Bob outlines ideas that he believes are involved in keeping music teachers and music students excited and involved in the music-learning process. The short version of the sequence adapted for our purposes works like this: The music teacher is motivated, at least in part, by selecting, teaching, and performing quality literature; music students, at least in part, are motivated by enthusiastic music teachers who provide quality music experiences for them through teaching, rehearsing, and performing quality literature; enthusiastic students who are excited about studying and performing quality music help make enthusiastic, involved parents; enthusiastic, involved, and informed students and parents help make happy, involved administrators; happy administrators support the quality program, and everyone is part of an informed, involved community that understands the value of music. An enthusiastic, prepared teacher, enthusiastic students who are involved in learning, quality literature, carefully planned teaching, and an informed support group are all an important part of this motivational interaction sequence; while nothing is really new here, the ideas are worth reviewing.

Planning for Success

An enthusiastic, prepared music teacher has often developed a philosophy for personal and program success. Jim Swearingen, Professor of Music Education at Capital

University and well-known composer, suggests a five-step procedure for developing a successful philosophy.

1. Start by observing others.

2. Communication is an absolute must.

3. Anything good takes time.

4. You need to be the role-model of your philosophy.

5. Be prepared to change your philosophy.

For Jim,

an outstanding rehearsal starts with an outstanding teacher.

In other words, the educational attitude that is reflected on the podium will have a tremendous effect on the success or failure of the conductor's rehearsal time.

An outstanding rehearsal starts with an outstanding musician.

A thorough knowledge of music, as it pertains to music performance, is an attribute that every conductor should possess.

An outstanding rehearsal can be achieved if your people skills will allow you to relate to your students in a highly positive manner.

Finally,

an outstanding rehearsal is well organized and planned in advance.

Quality Music

Planning for a successful rehearsal requires both a knowledge of quality teaching materials and a strategy for successfully teaching the material selected within the time available. We have been fortunate to have frequent guest composers visit our campuses. Many of these composers have been music teachers who write music for large ensembles. They have suggested that making decisions about what music to study and perform are among the most important decisions that music teachers make. They have described quality music as *honest music, music of integrity,* and music that appeals to our *emotions and intellect.* As ensemble directors, we all must find the right balance between *appropriate* and *good* music as we define it for our programs. However, what we serve our students as part of their daily musical diet may go a long way towards helping us get them to the good stuff mentioned in Chapter 1. According to composer Mark Camphouse, "The music that you select is really the textbook that you will be sharing with your children. Do you want these to be well thought out textbooks, or basically, do you want them to be comic books? Would you want your son or daughter to be taking an English class — a writing class in junior or senior high — that basically used comic books as a textbook, or would you want something more enriching?"

Jay Gilbert, Chair of the Music Department at Doane College, has suggested four ways to find and identify quality literature:

1. Attend professional music conferences.

2. Attend concerts presented by elementary, middle school/junior high, high school, college/university, and professional colleagues.

3. Attend summer workshops and reading sessions.

4. Consult bibliographies, state and national music lists, discographies, and recordings.

Teaching Music

Determining the *how,* or strategies, that music teachers will use to teach the music selected may be dependent on several factors including the age and ability of students (starting where the students are), amount of time available to teach (schedule), and the musical and overall program goals and objectives of the music teacher (there's that philosophy idea again). Each of these factors, and many others, may be different in each teaching situation. However, according to Robert Garofalo in *Blueprint for Band,* one factor may be common to anyone teaching in a music performance program: *performing group participation has little effect on musical behavior other than the acquisition of performance skills, unless there is a planned effort by the teacher to enrich the performing experience with additional kinds of musical understanding.* Teaching for musical understanding and knowledge (about music), while teaching the performance skills necessary to perform the music, requires a **balanced approach**. If the band, orchestra, or choir does not sound good, then the band, orchestra, or choir does not sound good.

The idea of comprehensive musicianship is not new. However, sometimes as music teachers, we think that teaching the music and teaching about music in a performance setting must be an *either/or proposition* — you cannot do both well. It is at least worth considering, however, that teaching for student musical awareness, understanding, and application (transfer) of the *big ideas* (concepts) in the music during regular music rehearsals might actually improve the level of student performance. The key is to

teach musical concepts as a part of your regular rehearsal.

Getting Started

Getting started is often the most difficult part of an activity. Getting started requires that same music teacher desire and planning mentioned earlier. The musical concepts that are taught during rehearsal generally come from the music selected for rehearsal/performance. Think of a favorite musical selection written for a type of ensemble familiar to you. As you picture the musical score and hear the sounds in your head, think about all of the musical concepts that you could teach to an ensemble using that selection (you pick the level of the group). Your list of ideas might include ideas like:

• information suggested by the title of the work

- historical placement of the composition

- composer/arranger background

- melodic lines

- harmonic schemes

- rhythmic elements

- meter

- tempo

- expressive markings

- dynamic plan

- form/structure

- texture

- orchestration

- articulations

- style

- phrasing

- technical considerations (the list could continue)

The music, chosen by the music teacher for study and performance, becomes the textbook. Each of the ideas listed above, depending on the composition, could take 30 seconds or 30 minutes (or longer or shorter) to teach, and could be accompanied by student projects, student assessments, or not. The point here is that the music teacher gets to decide why, what, when, and how much to teach about any of these and other big ideas about the music and music in general within the context of a regular rehearsal. There may not be time to study every musical selection in the same detail. The music teacher, armed with the knowledge of what his/her students need at the time, gets to decide.

Building Resources

Sometimes having sample approaches, models, and/or resources for gathering information can make the rehearsal planning task a little less overwhelming. For Deborah Sheldon, a general teaching approach starts with planning that involves creating expectations, developing achievable goals, having a plan, and *keeping no secrets from your students*. Deborah's general *rehearsal plan* looks like this:

The Rehearsal Plan
Who & What

- What do you want students to accomplish?

- Be realistic — goals will depend upon time.

- What materials can help attain goals?

- Are the materials level-appropriate?

- What elements can be taught with these materials?

Where

- What can your students do right now?

- Where were they at the end of the last rehearsal?

- Be aware of your students' progress — evaluate.

When & How

- Utilize sequential procedure to achieve outlined goals.

- Develop a recipe written for your substitute.

- What will you do (be specific)?

- What will the students do (be specific)?

- Have you missed steps or made bad assumptions?

- When should each step occur?

- Avoid *backwards* teaching!

Evaluation

- Have students accomplished the outline goals?

- Listen, ask questions, have them demonstrate.

- Take stock so you can plan for tomorrow.

The *big ideas* contained in this one general rehearsal approach could be adapted to fit a variety of teaching situations.

Lesson Planning

All (well, at least most) music teachers admit to using some kind of lesson planning when preparing for rehearsal. The lesson planning process is once again personal — what works for you is what works for you. What **works** ranges from typed, scripted lesson plans (these really do exist) to yellow Post-it® notes stuck on a score in appropriate places, and everything in between.

What follows are selected forms to use for music analysis (getting to know the music), forms for developing instructional units (for long-term study), forms for lesson planning (preparing to teach) and forms for daily rehearsing (the everyday routine). They are presented here as models to be adapted to fit individual situations.

CMP Teaching Plan

Wisconsin Music Educators Association
Comprehensive Music Program

Title _____

Composer _____

Publisher _____

Voicing/Inst. _____

Date _____

Music Selection

- Reasons for choosing the piece

Analysis

- Type of piece
- Heart of this piece
- Musical elements

    Form (macro- and micro-)

    Rhythm

    Melody

    Harmony (counterpoint, etc.)

    Timbre

    Texture

    Dynamics

    Style

    Growth

- Musical/cultural traditions and historical connections
- Quality and accuracy of edition

CMP Teaching Plan Strategies/Assessment

Wisconsin Music Educators Association
Comprehensive Music Program

Outcome #1   * Underline verbs

Strategies

>   * Check learning modes:
>
>   * Perform * Create * Listen * Describe

>   A.

>   B.

>   C.

Outcome #2

Strategies

>   A.

>   B.

>   C.

Assessment   * Before * During * After

Literature Analysis Form

Mark Fonder, Professor of Music
Ithaca College, Ithaca, New York

Title _____

Composer/Arr _____

Date Published _____

Publisher _____

Approximate Duration _____

Level of Difficulty _____

Unusual range or technical considerations:

Musical Concepts: Me-Me-Ha-Me-Fo-Sty-Co

Medium
     Orchestration
     Texture

Meter
     Tempo
     Rhythms

Harmony
     Keys
     Intervals
     Chords
     Harmonic techniques

Melody
     Scales
     Intervals
     Melodic techniques

Form

Style
     Terms
     Articulations
     History of piece
     Information about era

Composer

Creative Project

Repertoire Evaluation Form

Jay W. Gilbert
Chair of the Music Department
Doane College, Crete, Nebraska

Time _____

Title _____

Publisher _____

Date _____

Composer _____

Composer Dates _____

Historical Period _____

Grade _____

Instrumentation

	___bn	___eu	___	_____
___pc	___cbn	___tu	___	_____
___fl	___asx	___cb	___	_____
___ob	___tsx	___tmp	___	_____
___eh	___bsx	___sd	___	_____
___cl	___hn	___bd	___	_____
___ac	___ct	___cym	___	_____
___bc	___tp	___bells	___	_____
___bcb	___tb	___ ___	___	_____

Level of Difficulty _____

Brass Ranges:	_____tp1	_____tp2
_____tp3	_____tp4	_____hn1
_____hn2	_____hn3	_____hn4
_____tb1	_____tb2	_____tb3
_____eup	_____tub	*Level*_____

continued

Repertoire Evaluation Form

continued

Unit 1: Composer

Unit 2: Composition

Unit 3: Historical Perspective

Unit 4: Technical Considerations

*Level*_____

Unit 5: Stylistic Considerations

*Level*_____

Unit 6: Musical Elements

*Level*_____

Unit 7: Form and Structure

*Level*_____

Conducting Concerns:

Unit 8: Suggested Listening

Unit 9: Bibliography

Adapted from: *Teaching Music through Performance in Band*
(GIA Publications)

Daily Lesson Plan
Performing Arts Class

Date _____

Class _____

Compositions _____
_____
_____
_____

Objectives _____
_____
_____
_____

Introduction/Warmup _____
_____
_____
_____

Teaching/Learning Strategies and Activities
_____
_____
_____

Assessment Strategies
_____
_____
_____

Rehearsal Summary/Closure
_____
_____
_____

Resources and Enrichment Activities
_____
_____
_____

Rehearsal Planning Form

Date _____

Class _____

Compositions _____

Announcements to Post and Rehearsal Line-Up of Selections

_____

_____

_____

Tuning, Warm-Up, and Technical Development

_____

_____

_____

Musical Concepts/Objectives

_____

_____

_____

Composition _____ Specific Rehearsal Outline
(pages, measures, what to rehearse,
how to fix, timeline, etc.)

Timeline	*Composition/Section/Measures*	*What to Rehearse/ How to Fix*

Summary

_____

_____

_____

Making Transfers

There are many published materials that could be used as places to start in developing personal teaching strategies: the *National Standards; Blueprint for Band; Teaching Musicianship in the High School Band;* and the *Teaching Music through Performance in Band* series are just a few (see the reference section at the end of the book for specific information and more resources). While many of these books have the word *Band* in the title, most of the ideas presented have transfer possibilities to a wide variety of performance situations. For any of these ideas to *take* however — to become more than a *we tried that once, and it didn't work* comment — music teachers need to make the strategies *fit* their situations, and then must be committed to finding ways to *make them work* with real students. In the words of Winston Churchill, "Never, never, never, never, never, never, never, give up!"

Just Teach Music

Right about now you may be thinking something like: where do these college folks in their ivory towers get off telling me how to teach! If you are thinking that, please stop! And, if you know where we can find a real ivory tower, we would like to know so that we can visit one sometime. **Teaching Music is teaching music.** We don't have the answers for your music program, you have the answers for your music program. However, as we continue to process the information that we have gathered from music teachers across the country during our scheduling research, we are seeing examples of teachers attempting to implement the *National Standards,* doing curriculum

planning that includes daily lesson plans and long-term
sequential planning, changing their rehearsal pacing to fit
new schedules, trying new teaching strategies to be able to
teach in varying time periods, and generally re-thinking
and re-inventing what they do to, for, and with the
students in their performance programs. Many of their
ideas follow in the next chapters. The search for ways to
just teach music continues.

Chapter Four

Descriptions of School Music Programs That Include Teaching and Scheduling Strategies

"Above all, try something."
— *Franklin D. Roosevelt*

Public school music teachers across the country are being challenged to make it work one music program at a time. What follows are descriptions of more than 40 school music programs provided by band, choir, and orchestra directors selected from more than 200 music teachers who are making it work. Funding for this project was provided, in part, by the MidWest International Band and Orchestra Board of Directors.

Peter R. Mauro, Director of Bands
Allentown High School, Allentown, New Jersey

1. **School Description:**

   - Grades 9-12.

   - Enrollment is 912.

   - Part of the Upper Freehold Regional School District.

   - Southeast of Princeton, New Jersey.

2. **Schedule Description:**

   - Block scheduling: four blocks per semester, two semesters per year.

   - 85-minute classes in band all year long.

3. **Description of Teaching Strategies:**

   - Students receive five credits per semester, which is a boost to their academic grade point average.

   - The period has allowed me extra time to perfect our performance, the students' understanding of the music, and polish technique and terminology.

4. **Assessment or Grading Strategies:**

   - Class is graded on progress, evaluation of music and method materials, rehearsal techniques, and cooperation.

   - Very little change from previous years (45 minutes).

5. **Alternative Scheduling Teaching/Learning Advantages:**

   - Better sounding band.

- Stronger embouchures.

- Better intonation.

- These benefits will be reaped only when you have the band members for the entire year at 85-minute periods.

6. **Specific Suggestions:**

- Insist on the band and choir classes continuing for the entire year, 85 minutes per period, both blocks.

7. **Additional Information:**

Most block scheduling will kill music programs. Work closely with your administrators! Get your parents involved in the decision making in order to back up the director.

Anthony Stevens, Band Director
Barnstable High School, Hyannis, Massachusetts

1. **School Description:**

- Enrollment is 1,750.

2. **Schedule Description:**

- Four-period day.

- Ensembles meet in block five: Band on the stage, Chorus in the cafeteria, Orchestra in the lecture hall.

- Students only permitted to be in two ensembles.

- Students receive one credit per semester.

- Students scheduled for three days each week.

- Two days only, those students not in other group.

- Musical course offerings: Music Theory I and II (on the books only), Music History (proposed but not implemented due to budget), Concert Band, Concert Choir, and String Ensemble.

- Extra curricular music activities: Marching Band, Color Guard, Jazz Band, Show Choir, and Vocal Jazz Ensemble.

3. **Alternative Scheduling Teaching/Learning Advantages/Disadvantages:**

Advantages:

- Hallways are quieter.

- Fewer discipline problems.

- 90-minute rehearsals allow more work to be done.

- Time can be spent on tuning and other concepts.

Disadvantages:

- Students have a lot of homework.

- Students with less ability have difficulty sustaining their attention.

- Some teachers teach three blocks in a row.

- Some academic classes run all year for 86 minutes.

- Foreign language requires study in two consecutive semesters.

4. Additional Information:

- Does not work for every subject.

- New requirements at the freshmen level are pinching the performing groups.

- The "smart" schools are moving to this gradually.

- The faculty had no in-service on using a 90-minute period.

Vincent Tornello, Director of Bands
Charlottesville High School, Charlottesville, Virginia

1. School Description:

Charlottesville High School is the only high school in a community of approximately 40,000 and has an enrollment of 1,100 students. The band program has existed since 1940, with three directors.

2. Schedule Description:

- Monday, Wednesday, and alternating Fridays (Orange)

    7:50- 8:40   Marching Band or Jazz Ensemble

    8:56-10:36   first period (O)

    10:46-12:16 second period (O)

    1:07- 1:54   third period (O/B)

    2:00- 3:30   fourth period (O/B)

- Tuesday, Thursday, and alternating Fridays (Black)

    7:50- 8:40   Marching Band or Jazz Ensemble

    8:56-10:36   first period (B)

    10:46-12:16   second period (B)

    1:07- 1:54   third period (O/B)

    2:00- 3:30   fourth period (O/B)

3. Description of Teaching Strategies:

- Keep the rehearsal moving, but paced (for endurance).

- Work on rhythm charts, scales, and literature.

- Continue to encourage students to practice when class does not meet.

4. Assessment or Grading Strategies:

- Students are graded on the following characteristics:

    Musical Contribution to the Group Attendance

    Practice Merits (hourly log)

    Musicianship Tests

    Extra Responsibilities and Honors

    Interest, Attitude, Conduct, and Responsibility

5. Alternative Scheduling Teaching/Learning Advantages/Disadvantages:

Advantages:

- Marching Band (fall) and Jazz Ensemble (winter, spring) meet daily.

Disadvantages:

- Previous year was alternating block, Monday through Thursday, and straight seven-period day on Friday. It worked better than the current schedule.

6. **Specific Suggestions:**

- Prepare ahead of time (in selecting program literature), allowing enough preparation time.

7. **Additional Information:**

The one day to see everyone is a definite plus. Unfortunately we do not have that day any longer.

Alida W. Menefee, Vocal Music Director
Coatesville Area Intermed. H.S., Coatesville, Pennsylvania

1. **School Description:**

- Enrolls 1,100 students in 9th and 10th grades only.

- Located 40 miles west of Philadelphia.

- Suburban school.

- 33% minority (Black, Hispanic).

2. **Schedule Description:**

- Six-day cycle.

- Handbells and Chorus meet three days per cycle, year long.

- Other music classes (Piano, Electronic Music, Theory, Music Appreciation) meet three days per cycle, one semester only.

3. Description of Teaching Strategies:

- Be sure to have enough material for 82 minutes.

- Vary techniques: rehearsal time, "stretch" time, stand, sit, move.

4. Assessment or Grading Strategies:

- Portfolio assessment with all three choral groups.

- For Handbells, performance-based assessment as well as concert participation.

- Chorus is graded on concert participation.

- For Keyboards, grade comprised of performance-based tests, written, theory books, and homework.

5. Alternative Scheduling Teaching/Learning Advantages/Disadvantages:

Advantages:

- More accomplished in 82 minutes.

Disadvantages:

- Time is long for 9th graders — attention span (especially in choral rehearsal) is limited.

6. Additional Information:

Be sure the copier works (for class materials, worksheets, etc.)!

Steve Benaszeski, Band and Choir Teacher
Cornell Jr./Sr. High School, Cornell, Wisconsin

1. School Description:

- Located in northwest Wisconsin in a small city.

2. Schedule Description:

- Modified Block:

  Day 1—periods 1-4

  Day 2—periods 5-8

3. Description of Teaching Strategies:

- Each 90-minute music class divided into thirds (three activities). For example:

  Sr. High Choir: First 30 minutes: intervals, vocal health, warm-up, scale study, ear training, music theory. Second 30 minutes: sight-reading. Third 30 minutes: refine concert repertoire.

4. Assessment or Grading Strategies:

- Daily rehearsal grade for each student.

- Weekly lesson grade.

5. Alternative Scheduling Teaching/Learning Advantages:

- Students have a day to practice their parts prior to the next rehearsal.

- Teacher has an extra day for planning.

- It becomes more difficult for students to "get out of" rehearsals that meet every other day.

Judy Harmon, Choral Director
East High School, Cheyenne, Wyoming

1. School Description:

East is one of two high schools in Cheyenne. Enrollment is 1,600 — the largest in the state of Wyoming. Students' families are from low to middle income.

2. Schedule Description:

- Alternating A/B, 90-minute block schedule.

- Students have eight classes with an additional option of taking an early morning class, which meets for 45 minutes before regular classes begin.

3. Description of Teaching Strategies:

- The trick in 90 minutes is to do lots of things:

sitting	laugh
standing	sight singing
sectionals	vocal techniques
rhythm work	breathing techniques

4. Assessment or Grading Strategies:

- Students are graded on attendance, performance, vocal skill improvement, written tests, music terms, how their voice works, and basic theory.

5. Alternative Scheduling Teaching/Learning Disadvantages:

- Performances are sometimes difficult when they occur on a day that you do not see students.

- Memorization is more difficult due to lack of daily reinforcement.

6. Specific Suggestions:

- Be sure to have enough planned and vary the activities.

- Give yourself one year before deciding if you like it or not.

7. Additional Information:

I love it and so do our students!

Gary McCarty, Band Director
Emporia High School, Emporia, Kansas

1. School Description:

- Enrollment is 1,400.

- School district enrolls 5,500.

2. Schedule Description:

- "Eight block — Seven credit."

- Students enrolled in seven classes.

- Four classes meet each day — alternating A/B.

- Third block is a seminar: homeroom, study hall, peer tutoring.

- On Friday, all eight meet.

- Musical course offerings: String Orchestra, two Concert Bands, Jazz Band, four Choirs, Class Guitar, and General Music.

3. **Alternative Scheduling Teaching/Learning Advantages/Disadvantages:**

Advantages:

- Long block of time lets the students get into the class more.

- Able to spend more time on concepts.

- Shorter periods on Fridays work well for closure.

Disadvantages:

- More planning is required when getting information out to students.

Steve Kuske, Director of Bands
Evergreen High School, Vancouver, Washington

1. **School Description:**

- Grades 10-12, secondary.

- Enrolls 2,500 students.

- One of two high schools in the district.

2. **Schedule Description:**

   - 4 x 4 block.

   - Music students who are in Symphonic Band or Wind Ensemble begin school at 6:55 a.m., which is 30 minutes before the rest of the students begin school.

   - The district provides busing for those music students who come early or stay late.

   - Wind Ensemble has band for 53 minutes and then goes to a "core" class for period 1B, which is a required class.

   - The band and "core" classes are three trimesters long instead of two, as in the regular block.

   - The district pays extra-duty contracts for these "core" teachers.

   - Music students who are in Concert Band have their "core" class for the first part of fourth period and then band for 4B. They are then bused separately.

   - Jazz Band meets at lunch.

3. **Description of Teaching Strategies:**

   - Same as before.

   - Assistant director does individual testing and sectionals.

4. **Alternative Scheduling Teaching/Learning Advantages/Disadvantages:**

Advantages:

- Only music students have a five-period day, thus eliminating the "I can't fit into my schedule" excuse.

- Music students end up with more credits because they are in class more time than regular students.

- Music students' schedules are registered first, giving them an advantage in getting the classes they want.

Disadvantages:

- Limits flexibility of moving students to other bands.

Elden Moates, Band Director
Fannin County High School, Blue Ridge, Georgia

1. School Description:

- Located in the north Georgia mountains.

- Our county shares a border with North Carolina and Tennessee.

- Enrolls approximately 900 students and is the only high school in the county.

- Almost no ethnic diversity.

- High dropout rate.

2. Schedule Description:

- Six periods per day, 55 minutes each.

- Two band classes: Symphonic Band and another band class, which does not always have full instrumentation.

3. **Description of Teaching Strategies:**

- Demanding performance schedule.

- Use a method book with both classes.

4. **Assessment or Grading Strategies:**

- Students have tests on etudes and scales.

- Live auditions and taped auditions are used for chair placements.

- Individual achievement is taken into consideration.

- Combined grade of practice and participation.

5. **Alternative Scheduling Teaching/Learning Advantages/Disadvantages:**

- We have used the same scheduling methods since I began teaching 22 years ago.

6. **Additional Information:**

My school system has repeatedly discussed block scheduling, and I have researched all resources to assess the overall benefit of this. I understand that this system of scheduling has damaged many performing arts programs and that many studies show, while it is easier for an academic teacher to teach, block scheduling does not always produce the desired educational outcome for the student!

Steve Massey, Band Director
Foxboro High School, Foxboro, Massachusetts

1. **School Description:**

   * Enrollment is 720.

   * School district enrolls 2,600.

2. **Schedule Description:**

   * Four-period day — 4 x 4 block semester only.

   * Performing groups meet every other day for the year.

   * Health, physical education, and group guidance are also offered every other day to match with those students not in band and choir. These are required courses.

   * Currently still have study halls but eventually these will be replaced by school-to-work initiatives done independently.

3. **Alternative Scheduling Teaching/Learning Advantages**

   * Improved attendance.

   * Neatness and cleanliness improved.

   * Increased number of students on the honor roll.

   * Small class load for teachers.

   * Smaller course load for students.

   * Like 85-minute rehearsals.

   * Feels more like a college band rehearsal.

- Promotes good preparation and attitude.

- No evident negative effects.

4. **Additional Information:**

   - The first reason to do this is when the staff agrees philosophically that students learn better in longer periods of time.

   - Schools that try to do block scheduling and eliminate study halls simultaneously appear to have more difficulty.

   - Do a lot of sectional work with students after school.

   - I like everything about this schedule. So far, the only people unhappy with this is parents. We are able to teach everything we are teaching in music better. More materials and more in-depth study. This new schedule increases the time we have with students. We increased our graduation requirements as well.

Glenn Patterson, Music Teacher
Francis Scott Key High School, Westminster, Maryland

1. **School Description:**

   - Enrollment is 1,002.

   - School district enrolls 25,000.

2. **Schedule Description:**

   - 4 x 4 plan for the school with an A/B schedule for music performing groups.

- Opposite music performing groups are courses that meet on an A/B schedule.

      Phys. Ed.   grades 9 & 10

      Health   grades 9 & 10

      Social Studies   grades 11 & 12

- Three of the four periods are on an A/B schedule.

- 9th Grade Band and 10-12th Grade Band (some ability grouping is possible), Chorus I (mixed chorus), Chorus II (mixed chorus), Advanced Chorus, Choral Ensemble (small select group), Jazz Ensemble, Orchestra (9-12), Music History (not enough enrollment to schedule this year), Music Theory (not enough enrollment to schedule this year).

- Marching Band and Color Guard both rehearse after school.

3. **Alternative Scheduling Teaching/Learning Advantages/Disadvantages:**

Advantages:

- Students can take music performing groups for one credit all year.

- Ability to be in two performing groups.

- Enrollments in music have been maintained.

Disadvantages:

- Still unknown whether A/B maintains music skills to the same degree as meeting daily.

4. Additional Information:

- The instrumental program has grown considerably in the last three years. Expanding the schedule to include eight credits a year has helped make this possible.

- The key to our success has been a supportive administration that has wanted to maintain a quality program.

- We have one high school in our district on a standard 4 x 4 schedule and they are currently down 48% in band enrollment over a three-year period. They are now going to try to do some A/B to revive the program.

- Academic teachers who agreed to the A/B schedule went into it in order to maintain the music program.

Debbie Aurelius-Muir, Music Teacher
Franklin Magnet Middle School, Champaign, Illinois

1. School Description

Even though the school is a "magnet" school, all neighborhood children are accepted if they apply. All remaining children of the district must turn in an application and are then chosen by a lottery system. The school is located in an old part of town in a lower middle class area.

2. Schedule Description:

- I see all 6th graders for one quarter a year.

- 7th graders have two options — they may choose one quarter or one semester.

- 8th graders can choose not to have music (only 20% are allowed this option, the other 80% have it either all year or one semester).

- When a student is enrolled in music, we meet every day. Last semester, we tried only 6th graders coming to music for an equivalent of two class periods every other day (1 period = 42 minutes).

3. **Description of Teaching Strategies:**

I always begin class with a listening selection while I take attendance and the students get their materials out. They are instructed to listen to something specific. I try to make sure they respond physically to something every day, e.g., echo clapping, stretching, warming up muscles to music, singing, or instrumental playing. I bring in guest performers and have our own students perform. I ask students to lead physical warm-ups and to give presentations.

4. **Assessment or Grading Strategies:**

- Written notes recorded in a daily journal.

- Performances of vocal solos, dances, microphone skills, instrumental solos.

- Listening tests.

5. **Alternative Scheduling Teaching/Learning Advantages/Disadvantages:**

Advantages:

- Can assess everyone in one day.

- Can explain a project and have time to work on it in one class period.

Disadvantages:

- It is hard to keep kids involved for 80 minutes.

- If you are absent one day, you have missed two days.

6. Specific Suggestions:

- It takes a big adjustment to the lesson plans.

- Pacing is very important — plan activities in increments of 20 minutes.

- The third activity should involve movement — big or small.

7. Additional Information:

End-of-the-day blocks are a disaster — get as many adults in there as possible to bring down group size.

Rob Carroll, Band Director
Great Bridge High School, Chesapeake, Virginia

1. School Description:

Great Bridge High School houses 1,800 students in grades 9-12. Twenty percent of the student population is enrolled in the music program. The school is located in Tidewater, Virginia. The students are primarily from middle class, suburban homes.

2. **Schedule Description:**

- Six-period schedule with two alternating blocks per day.

- Students have an option to take a "zero" bell class before the regular school day.

3. **Description of Teaching Strategies:**

- Cooperative learning stressed.

- Concert Band rehearsals are quite conventional, meeting each day for 50 minutes.

- Listening, questioning, and constructivist techniques used.

4. **Assessment or Grading Strategies:**

- City-wide grading policy in effect for band grades 9-12:

    60%: Performance

    30%: Tests and Other Assignments

    10%: Instrument Inspection

- There are a minimum of three performance tests and one performance each nine weeks.

5. **Alternative Scheduling Teaching/Learning Advantages/Disadvantages:**

Advantages:

- Younger students (grades 9-10) are often better served by shorter class periods.

- Longer rehearsal time with the Symphonic Band (mostly grades 11-12) is a big success, allowing time to work more in depth and have a varied lesson plan to do more listening and evaluation.

- Allows a wide variety of activities and time for setup with Percussion Ensemble.

Disadvantages:

- Many teachers are using the block inefficiently.

- The consistency of everyday rehearsals is more advantageous for Concert Band.

6. **Specific Suggestions:**

- Ask yourself what is best for your students.

- Ask yourself what is best for your program.

- What do you need to do to make it happen?

- Become proactive in helping the administration design a schedule that best meets the needs of your students.

7. **Additional Information:**

Our school will make a decision June 1 as to what type of schedule we will use for the coming years. This is our third year on alternating block. I am working closely with our administration in designing the schedule.

Susan Adams, Choral Director
Gulfport High School, Gulfport, Mississippi

1. School Description:
   • Large high school with enrollment of 2,309.
   • The area is very pro arts.
   • We have active instrumental, choral, visual arts, and drama departments.
   • Our music organizations have held superior records for many years.

2. Schedule Description:
   • Full block or 4 x 4.
   • 90-minute classes, five days a week, four classes per day.

3. Description of Teaching Strategies:
   • Because we now have flexibility in the classroom, we now have time to teach the subject, not just from one performance to the next.
   • We use pacing guides to break down the 90 minutes into 30-minute segments to teach sight-reading, section rehearsals, Music History, etc.
   • Some periods are devoted to full rehearsal with a 30-minute lunch break.
   • Rehearsal is often done before lunch so when the choirs return, we can use CDs, tapes, etc. to listen critically to ourselves or example groups, or we can watch videos on vocal production or lives of composers, etc.

4. **Assessment or Grading Strategies:**

- Written assignments for class time and homework.

- Assignment of daily performance grades by individual and by section.

- Concert appearances and competitions are counted as major unit test grades.

5. **Alternative Scheduling Teaching/Learning Advantages/Disadvantages:**

   Advantages:

   - I find no *major* disadvantages.

   Disadvantages:

   - The only problem we have is coordinating the 4 x 4 plan with middle and elementary school schedules.

6. **Specific Suggestions:**

- You must be creative.

- Use student participation in leadership positions.

- The more the child participates, the easier the instruction becomes.

7. **Additional Information:**

- Teenagers become vocally tired so don't try to rehearse the whole period.

- You must organize your time as well as the students' time.

- Keep variety moving throughout the period.

- Once students and teachers adjusted, we would never return to a six-period day.

William J. Naydan, Director of Choral Activities
Hatboro-Horsham High School, Horsham, Pennsylvania

1. School Description:

- Located about 20 miles north of Philadelphia.

- Suburban school district of mixed race and socioeconomic levels, mostly middle to upper middle class.

- Enrolls approximately 1,400 students, grades 9-12.

2. Schedule Description:

- Modified block schedule.

- Four periods per day with a 75-minute study/activity period in the middle.

- Music classes meet 83 minutes each day and students have health and physical education mixed into their schedule.

- Students have band or choir either three, four, or five days a week all year, depending on their individual semester schedule.

3. Description of Teaching Strategies:

- Since going to the block, we now offer more electives and our enrollment has increased. I find much more time to work on musical subtleties, and we either sight-read or prepare more music than we actually perform.

- I have five small ensembles that meet once a week during the activity time. In addition, I run vocal sectionals for 25 minutes per voice part each week.

- I record all sessions, and students who need supplementary work make copies of the rehearsal tapes.

- I also use a monthly calendar and a daily message board to keep students aware of information they need to get, which I might forget because I see different students each day.

- I also use MIDI files to prepare students on their vocal parts.

4. **Assessment or Grading Strategies:**

- Students are graded in quartets each marking period or more often as time permits.

- Students are recorded singing in groups, each on a microphone.

- Assessment of students during class on a daily basis, having some sing individually or in sectionals.

5. **Alternative Scheduling Teaching/Learning Advantages/Disadvantages:**

Advantages:

- Students want to learn more music. I find myself singing almost twice as much literature as I can perform, which helps their general musicianship and strengthens their sight-reading abilities.

Disadvantages:

- The disadvantage is that I do not meet the entire choir unless I schedule a mass rehearsal; approximately four or five are scheduled before a performance. The five-day students sometimes become frustrated when we, out of necessity, need to review music for the students who are only there three times a week.

6. Specific Suggestions:

- Find a way to get as much on the schedule as possible and to somehow provide a year-round instruction — even if this means not meeting every day. A rotation could provide this if you have multiple ensembles.

- Also, do not be afraid to work on music for educational purposes only and not for performance. You can expand the choir's musicianship by doing many and various works with them.

7. Additional Information:

Find out what your kids want to study in your specific building and offer what they will take for electives. You cannot take someone else's successful model and make it work in your situation. You must create your own system from the ideas you have gotten from successful programs.

Bill Witcher, Band Director
Hibritten High School, Lenoir, North Carolina

1. School Description:

- Located in the rural mountains of North Carolina.

- Grades 9-12.

2. **Schedule Description:**

   - Concert and Symphonic Bands.

   - Pedagogy class for advanced students.

   - Class periods are 90 minutes each.

3. **Description of Teaching Strategies:**

   - Sectionals — first 30 minutes of each class.

   - Every student has an assigned day to play off either a Prescott Outline or concert music assignment.

   - Full band rehearsal lasts 60 minutes of class.

4. **Assessment or Grading Strategies:**

   - One point per day for class participation.

   - 8-10 points for weekly assignment.

   - Grading periods are six weeks each.

5. **Alternative Scheduling Teaching/Learning Advantages**

   - Get to hear every student play individually once a week and still have a 60-minute rehearsal every day.

6. **Specific Suggestions:**

   If one has the facilities, incorporate some type of similar schedule of sending students to sectionals.

7. **Additional Information:**

   We have the typical course conflicts of a small school on a four-period day.

David Enloe, Band Director
Hickory High School, Chesapeake, Virginia

1. School Description:

- Enrolls 1,850, grades 9-12.

- Community with strong parental support.

- Orchestra, 81; band, 159; chorus, 120.

2. Schedule Description:

- Modified block.

3. Description of Teaching Strategies:

- Begin with scales and sight-reading exercises.

- Rehearse compositions with a stretch break midway through class.

- Just purchased Vivace; building a Solo & Ensemble library which will be used during class time.

4. Assessment or Grading Strategies:

- Playing tests recorded on cassette tapes.

- Grade is:

    40% participation

    30% performance

    20% written exam

    10% after school sectionals.

5. **Alternative Scheduling Teaching/Learning Advantages/Disadvantages:**

Advantages:

- I see the kids longer.

Disadvantages:

- Continuity is affected.

- When students are absent for illness, holiday, or assemblies, there is too much time between class meetings.

- Last ten minutes are difficult at times.

6. **Specific Suggestions:**

- Pacing is a concern within the block and also a concern when preparing for a performance.

- Don't be opposed to starting your music too early, but don't be afraid to take time on scales, rhythms, chorales, and sight-reading. The extra time in the block is helpful in the long run when considering these factors.

Laura McBride, Director of Bands
Jeb Stuart High School, Falls Church, Virginia

1. **School Description:**

- Most culturally, racially, and economically diverse school in Fairfax County: 32% gifted, 11% learning disabled, and the rest are identified as ESL (English as a Second Language).

- Student population represents 60 countries and 130 different languages.

- Enrolls 1,320 students in grades 9-12 of which one-third are Hispanic, one-third are Asian, and the remainder are white, black, and Middle Eastern.

2. Schedule Description:

- Modified block.

- 100 minutes per class; first, third, and seventh on red day; second, fourth, and sixth on blue day.

- Fifth period meets each day for 48 minutes.

3. Description of Teaching Strategies:

- Playing tests on scales each day (major, minor, chromatic, arpeggios, and major thirds).

- Sight-reading.

- Sectionals.

- Guest conductors.

- Music listening.

- Class discussion of form, theory, and history.

- Ed Lisk "Circle of Fourths" warm-up plan.

- Rhythm studies (count and clap).

4. Assessment or Grading Strategies:

- Combination of rehearsal conduct, performance skills, and attendance.

- Extra credit given for concert attendance, short reports on a composer, or article from a magazine.

5. **Alternative Scheduling Teaching/Learning Disadvantages:**

- Poor retention level, especially for younger players.

- Difficulty with administrative affairs (i.e., collecting money, fees, forms, distributing travel information).

6. **Specific Suggestions:**

- Utilize resources (recordings, piano).

- Do more warm-ups.

- Use Gar Whaley's rhythm method, *Basics in Rhythm,* and have everyone count and clap.

- Have an announcement board posted or a white board for two-week schedule.

- Encourage students to stop by the band room on their "day off" to check announcements.

Bill Gibson, Music Director
Kingswood Regular H.S., Wolfeboro, New Hampshire

1. **School Description:**

- Facility houses 800 students in rural New Hampshire.

- Located in the Lakes Region (or middle part) of the state.

2. **Schedule Description:**

   • Modified block with four 90-minute periods.

   • Two of the 90-minute blocks are interrupted by a bell to allow some students to change classes (45-minute periods).

3. **Description of Teaching Strategies:**

   • Rehearsals are the same as they were in the past due to the fact that performing ensembles are scheduled during one of the split blocks (only 45 minutes).

4. **Assessment or Grading Strategies:**

   • Same as with regular schedule.

5. **Alternative Scheduling Teaching/Learning Disadvantages:**

   • Experimented with rehearsals on alternating days for 90 minutes all year long; the negatives outweighed the positives.

6. **Specific Suggestions:**

   Be aggressive when dealing with those who make the schedule! Stay involved with any committees devoted to schedule changes because they will affect the music class.

7. **Additional Information:**

   The everyday contact at this level is essential, I believe.

Jim Howell, Band Director
LaGrande High School, LaGrande, Oregon

1. School Description:

- School population of 900-950; only high school in town.

- Town population around 12,000, relatively isolated from any other towns of size — the two nearest towns of the same size are 45 miles in either direction.

- There is a small state university here which adds a lot to the town.

- Some drug problems, but less than average. No gang-related problems.

2. Schedule Description:

- Four classes per day, every day, for a semester.

- Music and a few other classes meet every other day, all year.

- The key here is to offer some required classes opposite music, as music students tend to be elective-rich. Freshmen can take PE alternating all year with either band or choir. Sophomores can take the state-mandated Personal Finance/Careers class. Juniors and seniors have a small variety of electives, can choose an open period, be a teacher's aide, or work out some other flexible option with individual teachers. Many teachers here will consider such flexible, individual study courses to facilitate serious music students. (Our block schedule was teacher driven and developed just before it became trendy).

- Classes are 88 minutes with eight minutes passing time and an hour lunch on Monday, Tuesday, Thursday, and Friday. Classes begin at 8 a.m. and end at 3:06 p.m. Teacher contract days are from 7:30 a.m.-3:30 p.m. The hour lunch was to facilitate individual student/teacher help and make-up, as missing a block for sports or illness can mean missing a considerable amount of teaching. Wednesdays have an altered schedule and are Faculty Forum about once per month and Teacher Access for the remaining time. Teacher Access is an additional chance for one-on-one help, designed for those who want and need it.

3. **Description of Teaching Strategies:**

- Maintain detailed rehearsal plans, which are kept on stand during rehearsal. Upon completion of rehearsal, mark progress on rehearsal plan and record unplanned learning experiences and topics which will be addressed in the next rehearsal.

- Train band to adjudicate recordings of fine ensembles by Oregon Band Directors Association scoring guides as well as their own performance tapes before hearing judges' scores (remarkable consistency here).

- Gradually introducing a four-year curriculum that requires components from Music Theory, Music History/Literature, and Performance.

- Ten to 15 minutes of each 88-minute Jazz Ensemble rehearsal is spent improvising on the Bb blues scale, includes conversations and experiments on the fundamentals of harmony and improvisation.

- Students must turn in a required jazz-listening list every three weeks, with increased detail after their first year in the class.

4. **Assessment or Grading Strategies:**

- Once a year, students write a formal, in-depth essay reviewing four other high school band performances at a non-competitive band festival using the English department's "process-writing" in which students turn in all drafts, plus peer-edited copy with the final.

- All are responsible for 70 common musical terms.

- Students must earn a modicum of points-per-quarter, outside of any events which I require, with other musical or artistic (dance, etc.) groups, and by attending concerts.

- Freshman Requirements: all major scales from memory; cycle of fourths (be able to write and identify as well as perform)

- Sophomore Requirements: natural minors

- Junior Requirements: must write and identify written intervals; may choose to do a performance at Solo/Small Ensemble contest *or* a well prepared presentation to the class on a composer (selected from my list), their life, music, and place in historical setting, including a short tape of representative excerpts

- Senior Requirements: aural recognition; must prepare a score and conduct a piece of easy band literature

- Percussionists (in separate ensemble class): responsible for all rudiments (over four years), in addition to the same requirements as the others; responsible for compendium of common percussion terms in German, French, and Spanish

- First Year Jazz Ensemble Players Requirements: major scales; cycle of fourths to the ninth, plus arpeggios

- Second Year and Above: ii-V-I scale progressions; cycle of fourths with arpeggios; all scales from memory

6. **Specific Suggestions:**

- Go in with a positive manner as a team player and get what you need for your program.

- Try for clarity on the issue that change should not negatively impact any educational program, and therefore must at least have parity for music with the existing schedule's opportunities.

- Be not afraid of stiff requirement in electives!

7. **Additional Information:**

I believe that the block schedule has gotten a bad reputation for many reasons. Part of this is obviously justified, but not inherently in the schedule, inasmuch as the administrative design and implementation — many of these flaws could antagonize music programs when shifting to *any* schedule. If the program is not defended, understood, and supported by those in power, it will have problems. Does the program deserve academic support? (You know that in many cases this is not so, and not required by districts and evaluators to be so; therefore, spiraling downward).

In other words, many of the problems that surface, or are exacerbated when shifting to a block schedule, have been there all along. There are many problems with a seven-period day, which are invisible because they are so familiar (so many that, looking back, I would not want to do 48- to 50-minute classes ever again).

Hilary S. Holmes, Band Director
Laramie High School, Laramie, Wyoming

1. School Description:

   • Albany County School District 1 is made up of five elementary schools, junior high school, and senior high school.

   • High school consists of 950 students, grades 10-12.

   • Located next to the University of Wyoming.

2. Schedule Description:

   • Modified block (periods 1-4 and 5-7 are on alternating days).

   • Block 1 is Concert Band (7:55 a.m.-9:30 a.m.).

   • Block 2 is Jazz Band (9:30 a.m.-11:05 a.m.).

3. Description of Teaching Strategies:

   Concert Band and Wind Ensemble:

   First 20 minutes — scales, long tones, and theory.

Rehearsal focuses on two compositions (first day work on notes and rhythms; next day review and move on to phrasing, dynamics, and tone).

Allows time for questions between pieces. Plan to incorporate history and theory into daily lessons.

Jazz Band:

Warm-up on scales, rhythmic patterns, and tuning.

15-20 minutes spent on each chart.

Break down problematic passages.

Theory is incorporated into the rehearsals.

4. **Assessment or Grading Strategies:**

- Each class is responsible for all scales (maj./min.) Scale tests are taped and critiqued.

- Playing tests every other week derived from folder music.

- Students receive points for having a pencil at rehearsal.

- Each class has student projects to do. Concert Band was responsible for writing a short, 10-measure piece of music in four-part harmony. Wind Ensemble will be researching the composer, R. Vaughan Williams.

- For each group, I try to pick a variety of styles and genres of music to play. I also combine the bands to work more in depth.

5. **Alternative Scheduling Teaching/Learning Advantages/Disadvantages:**

Advantages:

- More rehearsal time which facilitates more learning.

- Ample time for classroom discussion.

- Students play better.

Disadvantages:

- Kids becoming burnt out with too much playing.

- Concentration problems.

6. **Specific Suggestions:**

- Always have enough material prepared.

- Write every lesson plan; it will make your job much easier and things will run smoothly.

Sandy Steele, Vocal Music
Laramie Senior High School, Laramie, Wyoming

1. **School Description:**

- Located in southeast Wyoming.

- Enrolls 890 students, grades 10-12 only.

- Only high school in city.

2. **Schedule Description:**

- Alternating block schedule.

- 90 minutes for all classes.

3. **Description of Teaching Strategies:**

- I use a wide variety — general rehearsal, small group work, individual presentations, and aural and written theory.

- The most important thing to know is that you can't wing it; you must plan for 90 minutes. You cannot rehearse for 90 minutes straight either, so you must include many activities and still stay on task. An additional consideration is memorization, since you do not have daily repetition.

- You can always be very thorough in any given rehearsal.

4. **Assessment or Grading Strategies:**

- Students are graded each quarter.

    200 pts.: attendance

    100 pts.: tests (quizzes, part tests, sight singing)

    50 pts.: projects (may select from five activities)

    100 pts.: each concert

5. **Alternative Scheduling Teaching/Learning Advantages/Disadvantages:**

Advantages:

- I love the 90 minutes — so much time to try new things, dress rehearse, etc.

Disadvantages:

- Continuity is lost with days in between. When a student misses class, it has much more impact than a traditional schedule.

6. Specific Suggestions:

Learn about all of the options. Know when your classes meet, how it impacts your performances, and what new teaching strategies you will need to learn and employ.

7. Additional Information:

I include leadership students to manage roll and records that are not private.

Kenneth M. Krause, Director of Bands
Lebanon High School, Lebanon, Pennsylvania

1. School Description:

- Public school district located in Lebanon City.

- Formerly industrial-based (steel industry).

2. Schedule Description:

- 4 - 80-minute class periods.

    1 - 40-minute lunch.

    1 - 40-minute flex period (homeroom).

    3A - Choir (40 minutes).

    3B - Lunch (40 minutes).

    3C - Band/Orchestra (40 minutes)

- The third period is divided into three 40-minute blocks for lunch and music ensembles.

3. **Description of Teaching Strategies:**

- Lessons are offered on a daily basis. Students attend one 20-minute lesson, once a six-day cycle. Theory classes (level I, II, and AP) are offered for 80-minute blocks. Utilization of harmonic theory, solfege, conducting, piano, and small ensemble performance.

4. **Alternative Scheduling Teaching/Learning Disadvantages:**

- Difficulty in getting students out of classes for lessons, combined rehearsals, and performances outside of school.

5. **Specific Suggestions:**

- Attempt to have music ensembles scheduled at lunch times.

- Schools rarely cancel lunch periods for anything.

6. **Additional Information:**

The high school has a full-time choral director, full-time instrumental director, and part-time orchestra director.

Rodney S. Miller, Orchestra Director
Lebanon High School, Lebanon, Pennsylvania

1. **School Description:**

- Located in central Pennsylvania.

- Approximately 1,000 students in grades 9-12.

- Music curriculum includes: Orchestra, Symphonic Band, Marching Band, Jazz Band, instrumental ensembles, Show Choir, Concert Choir, Chamber Singers, Spring Musical, Music Theory I & II, Music Appreciation, Music History, and Music Technology.

2. Schedule Description:

- Modified block.

- Performance classes are 40 minutes.

- Classes for music and remaining courses are 80 minutes every day for one semester.

3. Description of Teaching Strategies:

- Teachers utilizing 80 minutes are encouraged to use three or four different teaching strategies during the class — less lecture and more actively engaging students as learners.

Joseph Filio, Jr., Teacher
Liverpool High School, Liverpool, New York

1. School Description:

• 10,000 students, K-12 (11 elementary schools, three junior high schools, and one high school).

- Liverpool is a suburb of Syracuse.

2. **Schedule Description:**
   - Students have four classes one day and three the next with an academic advisement.
   - Each block is 84 minutes in length.
   - Classes are taken for the entire year.

3. **Description of Teaching Strategies:**
   - Spend more time tuning and executing balance exercises.
   - Split block to 42 minutes for lessons.
   - Meet with sections of the band during academic advisement.

4. **Assessment or Grading Strategies:**
   - 60% of grade is from lesson assessment.
   - 40% is a result of band participation.

5. **Alternative Scheduling Teaching/Learning Disadvantages**
   - Reduction of literature rehearsed due to schedule conflict with orchestra.
   - Increase in lesson size due to the amount of lessons I can get in.

6. **Specific Suggestions:**

   If you have academic advisement, make sure that you are free in order to spend the time working with sections of the band.

Kurt Chrisman, Orchestra Director
Mayfield High School, Las Cruces, New Mexico

1. **School Description:**
   - Enrollment is 1,800.
   - School district enrolls 17,000.

2. **Schedule Description:**
   - Four-period day, same daily.
   - 85 minutes each.
   - One single block lunch.
   - Zero hour varies in length: either 1 hour four days a week (1/2 credit); daily for 90 minutes (1 credit); or three days a week for 65 minutes (1/2 credit).
   - Music course offerings: Chamber Orchestra (zero hour), String Orchestra, two Concert Bands, Jazz Band (zero hour), and Music Theory, Select Choir, two Women's Choirs, Madrigal (zero hour).

3. **Alternative Scheduling Teaching/Learning Advantages/Disadvantages:**

Advantages:
   - Length of time per class is a big benefit.
   - Can get into subject more in depth.
   - Great for field trips.

Disadvantages:

- Limited number of choices for students during each semester.

- More scheduling conflicts, especially with advanced and honors classes.

4. Additional Information:

- Went from six credits possible each year to eight credits per year.

- Using a zero-hour option due to students participating in AP classes.

- Orchestra enrollment has maintained or increased. We're not sure how long this will last.

- Appreciate being able to do sectionals during the scheduled rehearsal.

- We have zero hour to avoid students dropping out of the program. However, Jazz Ensemble and Madrigal groups that meet during zero hour have to also perform in the other regular hour class.

- I'm frustrated with the zero hour class. We need to meet more than three hours a week. Next year, I think we'll meet daily.

- I find we are using more music. The kids get burned out on pieces if we spend too much time on a selection we are preparing.

Gary E. Hall, Music Chair/Band Director
Montezuma-Cortez High School, Cortez, Colorado

1. **School Description:**

   • Located in southwestern Colorado, a remote area next to a Ute Indian Reservation.

   • Enrolls approximately 1,000 students.

   • Not a very affluent population.

2. **Schedule Description:**

   • 4 x 4 block.

   • 90-minute classes, four classes per semester.

   • Blocks are divided so that the following courses may be taught: two Jazz Ensembles, Symphonic Band, Percussion Ensemble, Chamber Ensembles, Concert/Training Band, Piano, Music Theory, and Jazz Choir.

3. **Description of Teaching Strategies:**

   • Every day is a recruiting day with every student, articles about the value of music included.

   • Include activities to keep students involved (i.e., ensembles, trips, concerts, guest clinicians, concerts with other schools, honor bands).

   • Perform music of the highest quality.

   • Lots of parent communication.

   • Push students to audition for All-State group.

- Peer pressure is great! We always encourage our top older students to encourage their friends to stay involved.

- Make sure the experience is a successful one for the students.

David Bean, Band Director
Morrison High School, Morrison, Illinois

1. **School Description:**

   - Small rural high school of approximately 400 students, grades 9-12.

   - Located in a northwestern Illinois community of 4,600.

2. **Schedule Description:**

   - Eight block alternating A/B days.

   - Each block is 85 minutes.

   - Students take eight classes each semester.

   - Music courses include: two levels of Choir, Madrigal Singers, Concert Band, Music Theory, and Music Appreciation.

3. **Description of Teaching Strategies:**

   - Rehearsals must be paced differently with the heavy rehearsal loaded to the front, just after warm-ups.

   - During the middle of the rehearsal, a five- or ten-minute period is used for instruction in theory, history, or background information on the piece or composer.

- For more continuous playing, the end of the rehearsal is saved for pieces that are closer to completion in the rehearsal cycle.

4. **Assessment or Grading Strategies:**

- Both band and choir use a portfolio grading system.

5. **Alternative Scheduling Teaching/Learning Advantages/Disadvantages:**

Advantages:

- Extra period has increased enrollment in performance and non-performance music classes.

Disadvantages:

- Less overall instructional time than our previous schedule (75 minutes less class time every two weeks than previous seven-period day schedule).

6. **Specific Suggestions:**

Handling the management details of an active music program in an every-other-day setting is difficult. It requires the teachers to be more organized and plan farther ahead.

Dave Leonard, Orchestra Director
Neenah High School, Neenah, Wisconsin

1. **School Description:**

- Enrollment is 2,000.

- School district enrolls 7,000.

2. **Schedule Description:**

- Five-period trimester — 70-minute periods.

- Freshman Band and Orchestra meet first hour.

- 10th-12th Grade Band and Orchestra meet fourth hour.

- Choirs meet every hour.

- Lunch is in the third hour (220 minutes — 30 minutes for lunch — only one choir meets in this area).

- Leaves a 90-minute period (20 minutes recommended for study time).

3. **Alternative Scheduling Teaching/Learning Advantages/Disadvantages:**

Advantages:

- Team teaching.

- Longer periods.

- Can do more than just prepare for the concert.

Disadvantages:

- 10th-12th grades are only in one group. Although a student could take two, presently not a single student does because it would take up 40% of their schedule.

- Some students are not participating in all three trimesters.

4. **Additional Information:**

- We are working on changing the schedule so that 10th-12th graders can be in more than one performing group. This would require using our rehearsal rooms effectively. You have to have the space to do this.

- Require students to participate in two trimesters.

- We strongly recommended all three trimesters. However, students are required to take at least two.

- Overall, enrollment increased in all three music areas this year.

- The Board of Education committed to making no reductions in staff. The music department was part of this change.

- Not all music directors are happy with sharing students that meet in the same period (i.e., 9th grade).

Nathan Wright, Choral Music Director
Northridge High School, Layton, Utah

1. **School Description:**

- Located 25 miles north of Salt Lake City in Layton, adjacent to Hill Air Force Base.

- Currently enrolls 2,000 students in grades 10-12.

2. **Schedule Description:**

- A/B block schedule; four 85-minute periods each day.

- Two semester blocks per year, 90 days per semester.

3. Description of Teaching Strategies:

- One-third class spent warming up.

- Remainder of class spent rehearsing.

4. Assessment or Grading Strategies:

- Assessment/Grading strategies not affected by schedule.

Charlene Toler, Band Director
Ozark High School, Ozark, Missouri

1. School Description:

- Ozark is a rapidly growing community in south central Missouri, located between Springfield and Branson.

- Enrolls about 950 students, grades 9-12.

Gail McGinnis, Choir Director
Petal High School, Petal, Mississippi

1. School Description:

- Enrollment is 1,030.

- School district enrolls 5,000.

2. Schedule Description:

- Modular schedule.

- Seven periods, including two alternating blocks.

- Band meets every day (50 minutes).

- Choir meets three days per week for 84 minutes.

- Musical course offerings: two SSA 9th Grade Women's Choruses, Concert Choir, SSA Show Choir, Mixed Show Choir, Band, and General Music.

- Extra curricular musical activities: Madrigal, Vocal Sextet, Vocal Quartet, Marching Band, and Jazz Band.

3. **Alternative Scheduling Teaching/Learning Advantages/Disadvantages:**

Advantages:

- Students like not having to do homework every night.

- Principals believe the teaching is better.

- Longer periods require a variety of activities.

Disadvantages:

- Not seeing students every day.

- Too much of a tech-prep emphasis.

- Being creative enough to keep kids focused.

4. **Additional Information:**

I'll take this any day over a 4 x 4 plan!

Terry Ingram, Band Director
Petal High School, Petal, Mississippi

1. **School Description:**

   - Suburb of Hattiesburg, which is located in south Mississippi.

   - Hattiesburg is a town of about 60,000 people and Petal's population is approximately 12,000.

   - Enrolls 1,031 with approximately 90% of the student body being white, middle class.

2. **Schedule Description:**

   - Modular block with first and seventh period meeting every day.

   - Band is first period. All other blocks meet three days a week for 84 minutes.

3. **Description of Teaching Strategies:**

   - Since band meets every day for 64 minutes, I haven't made any changes from the typical six- or seven-period schedule.

   - In addition to curricular rehearsal time, all band students spend four hours per week in after-school rehearsals.

4. **Assessment or Grading Strategies:**

   - Performance grades.

   - Tryout grades.

   - Attendance at all rehearsals.

- Students turn in cassette tapes for grades and also receive much input in private lessons (about 50% of our students study privately).

5. Alternative Scheduling Teaching/Learning Advantages:

- The block schedule has not changed the teaching/learning experience because band meets every day for 64 minutes.

6. Specific Suggestions:

The music program at our school involves approximately half of the student body. Many of these students are involved in both band and choir. Our administration has discussed the 4 x 4 schedule. The music faculty has tried to gather information to make educated decisions and to also keep the administration informed as to the effect the 4 x 4 would have on our programs.

7. Additional Information:

Our middle school 7th graders have had band three days a week for 72 minutes the past three years because of scheduling. This year the classes are meeting five days a week for 42 minutes and are much more successful.

Charles Bolton, Band Director/Dept. Chair
Sam Barlow High School, Gresham, Oregon

1. School Description:

- Located 20 miles east of Portland.

- Enrolls 1,800 students, grades 9-12.

- 260 students enrolled in five band classes.

- Two directors.

2. **Schedule Description:**

- Traditional seven periods on Monday; modified block schedule for remainder of the week.

- Classes meet three times per week (twice for 83 minutes and once for 44 minutes for a total of 210 minutes per week).

3. Description of Teaching Strategies:

- The period is split into thirds: The first portion of the class is used for warm-ups, scales, rhythm exercises, and tuning. Slower music, chorales, the middle section of overtures, suites, etc. are played during the second portion of class. The final segment of class is reserved for light, up-tempo music.

- During rehearsals with the two younger groups, we also do some theory and conducting in the middle as a change of pace as well as to enhance their music education.

- Jazz Band spends time in the middle of the block listening to recordings or doing improvisation.

4. **Assessment or Grading Strategies:**

- Playing tests every six weeks.

- Semester playing exam.

- Written tests.

- Performances are required with an alternate activity available, if absence is excused.

- If student is ill or misses a number of classes, he may turn in a written report, help at the grade schools, or attend a concert and submit a critique.

5. **Alternative Scheduling Teaching/Learning Advantages/Disadvantages:**

Advantages:

- The older students do well with the extended periods. Most of the juniors and seniors study privately and practice semi-regularly.

Disadvantages:

- Younger students and those not as dedicated seem to have a high dropout rate.

- When you can teach the students five days per week, all will make some progress, but two to three days a week is not enough.

6. **Specific Suggestions:**

The bottom line is this: any schedule that allows students to take electives will work; some better than others. However, some schools have schedules that limit electives. If the schedule allows all students to be in band, the director, students, and parents can make it work.

7. Additional Information:

- Teaching basics such as rhythm, notes, etc. is even more important than before. Students must be able to read music because there is less time to reinforce.

- We also have a Jazz Band "0" period at 6:40 a.m. every day. It is a big help because the top players are playing five days a week, which produces good chops.

Paul Phorpe, Music Teacher
Skyline High School, Longmont, Colorado

1. School Description:

- Enrollment is 1,100.

- School district enrolls 16,995.

2. Schedule Description:

- five-period day — trimester.

- 70 minutes each period.

- 50 minutes lunch.

- five minutes passing time.

- Music course offerings: Band, Jazz Choir, Mixed Choir, Women's Choir, Freshman Choir, Beginning Guitar, Intermediate Guitar, History of Rock & Roll, Jazz Improvisation.

- Jazz Ensemble meets during lunch hour (50 minutes).

- Pep Band is extra curricular.

3. **Alternative Scheduling Teaching/Learning Advantages/Disadvantages:**

Advantages:

- 70-minute rehearsals are great.

- Can teach more than getting ready for performances.

- Have more time for theory, ear training, etc.

Disadvantages:

- Limits the number of choices students have for classes.

- It is very difficult for students to be in two music performance groups.

4. **Additional Information:**

- Band program used to have 150 students enrolled before the five-period day was implemented. Currently there are about 100 enrolled.

- Students have difficulty staying in the program for four years, especially if they are college bound.

- Band and Orchestra are scheduled in the same period. This includes about 25 of the top players.

- There are three high schools, grades 9-12, and three combination middle and high schools. The three 9-12 high schools have three different schedules — all are some form of block (one A/B, one 4 x 4, one five-period trimester).

Stan McGill, Choir Director
South Garland High School, Garland, Texas

1. **School Description:**

   - Located in the northeast corner of Dallas-Ft. Worth Metroplex.

   - Enrolls 2,500 students (5A school).

   - 75% White, 15% Hispanic, 10% Afro-American.

2. **Schedule Description:**

   - Modified block, alternating A/B days.

   - Class periods are 90 minutes each.

   - Seven vocal classes.

3. **Description of Teaching Strategies:**

   - Daily warm-ups.

   - Variety in rehearsals.

   - Fast paced.

   - Communication (upcoming events, goals, etc.).

4. **Assessment or Grading Strategies:**

   - Spring tests.

   - Participation grades.

   - Sectional/Extra rehearsal attendance.

   - Concert grades.

5. Alternative Scheduling Teaching/Learning Advantages:

- Advanced placement/accelerated graduation tract.

6. Specific Suggestions:

- Make every rehearsal an "event" in itself due to planning prior to rehearsal.

Sam Elson, Music Teacher
Thomas Edison High School, Alexandria, Virginia

1. School Description:

- Enrolls 1,100 students.

- 110,000 students enrolled in the school district.

2. Schedule Description:

- four-period day.

- 90 minutes per class.

- seven minutes passing time.

- 25 minutes for lunch.

- Some courses meet daily for a semester and some meet every other day for the year.

- Music course selection: Symphonic Band, Concert Band, Beginning Band, Orchestra, Symphonic Choir, Edison Singers (select group), Women's Choir (spring semester only), Piano, Guitar, and Music Theory.

- Marching Band meets after school three times per week for 10 weeks. This is a requirement for Symphonic Band students.

- Jazz Ensemble meets after school.

3. **Alternative Scheduling Teaching/Learning Advantages/Disadvantages:**

Advantages:

- Allows time to rehearse music in depth.

- Our administrators have done a good job of making this work for music by making it year-long.

- Kids like having a day between every-other-day classes to prepare.

Disadvantages:

- Attention span becomes a problem.

- Younger students do not have physical endurance (i.e., trumpets).

- Less content is being covered in academic classes.

- Discipline is a problem in our school. Block scheduling may reduce discipline issues in the hallway, but not in the classroom.

- As a teacher, I am tired by the end of the third teaching hour.

- Students take a lot of AP courses.

- Combination of teaming and block scheduling at middle school level is taking toll on music enrollments.

Douglas C. Orzolek, Ph.D., Director of Bands/Music Chair
Thomas Jefferson High School, Bloomington, Minnesota

1. School Description:

- Student enrollment is 1,750 (500 in music), grades 9-12.

- 90,000 residents in the city that is located 10 miles south of Minneapolis.

- The band has traveled to all parts of the world, mid-west, state conventions, and marched in several major parades.

2. Schedule Description:

- Standard 4 x 4 block.

- Music classes last 90 minutes for entire school year.

- Music classes meet every day.

3. Description of Teaching Strategies:

- Rehearsals are limited to 60 minutes with 30 minutes designated for AMP class/sectional work.

- Each period looks similar to this:

  First 30 minutes: half of choir to AMP; half of choir in sectional; band has full rehearsal

  Second 30 minutes: full choir rehearsal; full band rehearsal

  Third 30 minutes: full choir rehearsal; half of band to AMP; half of band in sectional

4. Assessment or Grading Strategies:

- 25% music theory tests

- 25% quarterly solo or ensemble performance

- 25% music appreciation test

- 25% participation, playing quizzes, performance attendance

5. Alternative Scheduling Teaching/Learning Advantages:

We know more about what we are playing; therefore, we perform much better, while rehearsing the same amount of time as the seven-period day prior to the advent of the block.

6. Specific Suggestions:

- Educational reforms are just that — reforms. Reform means changing strategies, styles, and methods to suit the needs of the reform. Be flexible enough to meet those reforms without allowing the quality of education to dwindle.

- Educate yourself and then educate others!

7. Additional Information:

The AMP class integrates Music Appreciation, Music Listening, Music History, and Theory. The presentations are designed to be interesting and fun. The music faculty determined that a class with a broad range of topics and discussions would be most appropriate. In order to achieve these goals and to establish a model for such a class, the following areas of concern were determined to be important enough to include in each quarter that the class is taught.

Music Theory/Vocabulary

History of Music (Western/Non-Western)

Current Musical Events

Social and Cultural Issues Related to Music

Enhancing the Performance of Music

Guest Speakers/Performers

Careful and detailed study of a "Masterwork"

Discuss how music is reflective of life and society

Bruce Caldwell, Executive Manager/Retired Teacher
Washington Music Educators Assn., Edmonds, WA

1. School Description:

- Four-year high school in Seattle suburb.

2. Schedule Description:

- Three periods daily, alternating A/B, 100-minute classes.

- After three years, the school switched to four periods, A/B, 90 minutes.

3. Description of Teaching Strategies:

- Make activities relevant to the music (i.e., theory and history).

- Make the music being taught relevant to the learning desired.

- Do various things during the period (i.e., full band rehearsal, sectionals, seat work, leadership activities, etc.).

4. **Alternative Scheduling Teaching/Learning Disadvantages:**

   - Alternating days inconvenient for performing groups, especially near performance dates.

5. **Specific Suggestions:**

   - Do not go to 4 x 4 block!

6. **Additional Information:**

   The block isn't as much a problem as continuity from semester to semester. I'd rather have the kids every other day than every other semester.

Sandra Nicolucci, Ed.D., Director of Performing Arts (K-12) Wellesley Public Schools, Wellesley, Massachusetts

1. **School Description:**

   - Located approximately 12 miles west of Boston.

   - Affluent suburb, largely comprised of professionals.

   - Consists of six elementary schools, one middle school, and one high school.

   - Fine Arts faculty is led by two K-12 directors: visual and performing arts (drama, dance, music).

- Enrolls 3,300 elementary children, 650 middle school students, and 870 high school students.

- School budget is approximately $22 million.

2. **Schedule Description:**

- Seven-day cycle with some vertical rotation containing 60-minute blocks and one 100-minute block each day.

- Every subject gets one 100-minute block per cycle, including arts.

- There are dedicated elective periods at the extremes of the day and an "elective priority block" in the middle of the day wherein no academic singletons may be scheduled.

- Arts classes scheduled throughout the day.

3. **Description of Teaching Strategies:**

Performing Groups:

Use of student conductors to lead full ensemble

Use of section leaders to run sectionals

Use of time during 100 blocks to occasionally rehearse chamber groups

Viewing of videotapes of concerts for self-critique, according to rubrics

Listening to recordings of compositions to be performed

Non-performing Groups:

Lots of hands-on exposure to software, composing, arranging

Small groups discussions and problem solving

Presentation of projects, e.g., Hyperstudio stacks on jazz composers in "History of Jazz" course

4. Assessment or Grading Strategies:

We are currently studying authentic assessment in our K-12 and culled out the ones that appear to be the most authentic. For example, our culminating unit in 5th grade involves composing a piece of music in a cooperative group to demonstrate understanding of the elements of music, which have been taught in a sequential manner K-5. At the high school level, teachers are learning about defining rubrics for more objective assessment of performance. Currently, students and teachers view videotapes on concerts or rehearsals and assess the quality, according to general categories. However, the addition of specific rubrics will heighten awareness of nuance and foster much more analytical thinking about successful and unsuccessful aspects of performance. Some teachers are beginning to record rehearsals for the same purpose.

5. Alternative Scheduling Teaching/Learning Disadvantages:

Big disadvantage: you cannot share teachers among schools. We have dedicated elective blocks at the extremes of the school day. In the past, we have relied on the 7:25 a.m. block heavily because that was when we could get kids without conflicts. We would like to incorporate our courses more into the "real" school day and are implementing that much more this year. These extreme blocks are also shorter than the "normal" blocks so performing groups scheduled then are short-changed. We have moved many of our ensembles into the *Elective Priority (III) Block*. Concert Band, Concert Choir, and Orchestra (as of next year) meet then. This enables "cross-fertilization" among the groups, e.g., wind and percussion players can experience both band and orchestra, the chorus and orchestra can combine for "master works," etc. We love the long periods for rehearsals, especially the 100-minute block!

6. Specific Suggestions:

- Do not back down from having performing groups scheduled for the entire year.

- Advocate tirelessly for either dedicated elective periods or elective priority blocks without conflicts with singleton academics — *this is possible to schedule*.

- Advocate for the scheduling of cross-graded courses before academics are scheduled.

- Try to schedule major performing groups simultaneously in the same block, if space allows, so that students can experience more than one without "overloading" with arts electives.

7. Additional Information:

- The typical 90-minute period, four periods per day schedule model, can be death for music programs, especially the model that has two semesters. The four-period day model does not work well for the arts unless there is a split block.

• In the scheduling model we work under, we cannot easily share staff among buildings, which takes something away from our ability to "farm the vertical feeder system."

Tony Martinez, Band Director
Western Heights High School, Oklahoma City, Oklahoma

1. School Description:

• AAAA school with 800 students (grades 9-12).

• First suburb outside of Oklahoma City limits.

2. Schedule Description:

• Class meets every day of the year from 7:45 a.m. to 9:25 a.m.

3. Description of Teaching Strategies:

• Use extra class time for sectional work and individual help.

4. Assessment or Grading Strategies:

• Point system that awards students for participation and attendance of concerts and contests.

• Several playing tests are scheduled each week.

5. Alternative Scheduling Teaching/Learning Advantages/Disadvantages:

Advantages:

- Increased class time eliminates the need for most extra rehearsals and sectionals.

Disadvantages:

- Currently unable to fit Jazz Band and Music Theory into the schedule.

6. Additional Information:

Straight block scheduling seems to work better than modified block.

Greg Stepp, Band Director
Western Hills High School, Frankfort, Kentucky

1. School Description:

- Located in the state capital.

- One of two high schools in the county.

- Grades 9-12.

- Enrolls 850 students.

2. Schedule Description:

- Modified block, third block is split.

- Jazz Ensemble meets 50 minutes.

- Concert Band meets 50 minutes.

- Music Appreciation meets 90 minutes.

- Music Theory meets 90 minutes.

3. **Description of Teaching Strategies:**

   - Jazz Band and Concert Band are quick with planning for efficiency and broad approach since grades 9-12 are in the same class.

4. **Assessment or Grading Strategies:**

   - Playing tests.

   - Written assignments.

   - Motivation and participation are considered.

5. **Alternative Scheduling Teaching/Learning Advantages/Disadvantages:**

   Advantages:

   - 32-credit capabilities helps with new grade requirements.

   Disadvantages:

   - Some class conflicts are present.

6. **Specific Suggestions:**

   - Be flexible.

   - Look ahead.

   - Keep students in mind.

Glenn Patterson, Music Teacher
Westminster High School, Westminster, Maryland

1. School Description:
   - Enrollment is 2,200.
   - School district enrolls 25,000.

2. Schedule Description:
   - 4 x 4 plan for the school with an A/B schedule for music performing groups with other subject areas.
   - Opposite music performing groups, these courses also meet on an A/B schedule:

     | Phys. Ed. | grades 9 & 10 |
     | Health | grades 9 & 10 |
     | Social Studies | grades 11 & 12 |

   - Three of the four periods are on an A/B schedule.
   - Music course offerings: Concert Band (9th), Symphonic Band (9th-12th), Wind Ensemble (9th-12th select group), Chorus I, Chorus II, Advanced Chorus, Jazz Ensemble, Orchestra (9th-12th), Guitar, Piano, Music History, and Music Theory.
   - Marching Band and Color Guard both rehearse during and after school.

3. Alternative Scheduling Teaching/Learning Advantages/Disadvantages:

Advantages:

- Students can take music performing groups for one credit all year.

- Ability to be in two performing groups.

- Enrollments in music have been maintained.

Disadvantages:

- Still unknown whether A/B maintains music skills to the same degree as meeting daily.

4. Additional Information:

Music enrollments increased only in choir, others stayed even. Not all music faculty like meeting for 90 minutes every other day but some do.

Thomas Alderson, Teacher/Band Director/Dept. Chairman William Penn High School, New Castle, Delaware

1. School Description:

- Grades 9-12, comprehensive high school.

- Student population of 2,300 of which 55% are white.

- Primarily a blue-collar community that is a mixture of urban, suburban, and rural attendees.

2. Schedule Description:

- Seven-period day with 44 minute periods and five minutes of passing time.

• There are no blocked periods for music classes. The school has chosen to block only a portion of the classes and that may vary from one grade level to another. English and Math are blocked as well as Social Studies and Science. This permits an A/B alternating schedule.

3. Description of Teaching Strategies:

The state of Delaware has adopted a new curriculum for the visual and performing arts. As a result we are in a process of change requiring new approaches to the time we are allotted and the types of material that we are going to cover. In my own approach, I am laying out a program of study with the larger performing groups that will incorporate these skills over a period of four years, thus permitting the performance aspects of the curriculum to continue. The concept of performance, being interpreted as public performance, has changed. Performance now is intended as performance within the classroom. Performance in public is an added plus, which is not considered part of a grade (extra credit, maybe). We also labor under a Board of Education that has a policy of eligibility. If a student does not attain a certain GPA within a marking period, then the student is not eligible to perform or participate outside the normal school day in any activity whether it is extra curricular or curricular. Within my program, I incorporate theory concepts — counting in improvisation and composition. This is in addition to a concert schedule that includes a Holiday Concert and Spring Concert with appropriately challenging literature.

4. Assessment or Grading Strategies:

- Students are graded on:

    A. Written material in the form of tests, homework, and classroom assignments.

    B. Individual playing in the form of scale requirements up to 5#'s, 5b's, and chromatic. Percussion have, in addition, their 40 rudiments as well as their tuning skills.

    C. All students prepare and perform the All-State Solo for their peers/section members. If auditioning for All-State, the student plays for the entire group.

    D. Cassette tapes are submitted for assigned portions of their concert program for a grade.

5. Alternative Scheduling Teaching/Learning Advantages:

I have not changed my style of teaching as a result of schedule change.

6. Specific Suggestions:

Fight for a schedule that will allow year-long learning in the music program. There is a wide variety of material available, both within yourself and through outside sources, which will allow a tremendous amount of musical instruction to take place whether it is in a traditional setting or a block. Be creative and allow your students the ability to grow and experiment with improvisation, composition, singing, playing, sight-reading, listening, and evaluating performances of themselves and others.

Chapter Five

Creating Variety
In The Daily Rehearsal

"We will not know unless we
   begin."
                        — *Howard Zinn*

The daily rehearsal is generally a time of practice in preparation for performance. For most ensemble directors, the goal is to define the style, to repeat for precision, and to refine the expression. This rehearsal/practice process often leads to a "rehearse letter C" syndrome — every day being the same routine for each class, simply repeated ‖: over and over and over :‖ until the performance. The procedure is then re-started for the next performance, with new selections of course, and then repeated ‖: over and over and over :‖ until the performance. For the next year, new works are selected and the routine is simply repeated again.

Our research has identified strategies used by music teachers nationwide to create variety in their daily rehearsals. As one music teacher expressed "variety (in rehearsal), the spice of life — has been the factor to keep me charged and challenged." The following suggestions are offered as creative additions to your own rehearsal strategies leading to expressive and precise music making. As with any innovation or change of routine, some could easily exploit an idea and never achieve the intent of the performing arts class — *to perform.*

The 28 ideas that follow present ways in which the music teacher could have "special-emphasis days" to create variety from a normal and repetitive daily rehearsal.

Repetition Day

The objective of this strategy is to rehearse special sections in the music that require a great deal of repetition sequence to either develop consistency or precision. Individual measures, sections, or entire works could be the focus for the repetition. Some directors report that conditioning students for the needed repetition and devoting a special day stimulates a more favorable response and tolerance. This procedure is based on rote teaching, modeling, and/or drill. Caution is encouraged in order to avoid overusing or misusing this technique. The exploitation of this technique could lead to music illiteracy, lack of conception teaching, as well as music burnout.

Joseph Casey, in his book *Teaching Techniques and Insights*, indicates the following concerning the use of this procedure:

> Teachers usually use drill and repetition to develop the students' skills or facility, admittedly important gains; but students can actually gain much more from drill and repetition. Repetition can help students finger a difficult passage correctly or match the tone of a model. Students need repetition to learn to blend with the section, to phrase musically, or to read notation accurately. To improve upon any of these skills, the student must practice the actions repeatedly.[1]

Repetition day can include a variety of presentation methods:

- slow to performance level tempos

- use of the metronome (possibly amplified)

- loud and soft contrasts, as well as other expressive elements being focused

- (sections) woodwinds, brass, percussion, strings, sopranos, altos, tenors, basses, etc.

- (individuals) within a section

- repetition of rhythms, melodic, or harmonic sequences

- repetition of articulation, bowing, or diction concerns

Stop Day

This technique requires the conductor to stop at any point to correct errors or to deliver needed information. The approach usually involves conditioning the ensemble — only accuracy and precision of the section being rehearsed is satisfactory. When any error occurs, the director *immediately stops* and restarts. The director does not keep going in the music until the error has been corrected. Of course, the director would be expected to provide appropriate instruction/feedback for improved performance and/or to rehearse the needed section. Directors using this rehearsal technique report that their intention is to send the unquestionable message that "only accuracy and precision are acceptable for achieving musical excellence. Working towards perfection is the goal."

Sight-Reading Day

Ideally, sight-reading should be a part of each daily rehearsal. However, special days devoted to sight-reading reinforce and assist in the development of music literacy. The goal with all sight-reading should be to encourage all students to be able to read music independently and not to depend on rote or mechanical playing/singing.

When incorporating a sight-reading day, the director should use a consistent system of delivery. Directors could prepare music in advance, placed in special folders for distribution, time the amount of observation by the students and score study by the director, and outline the sight-reading steps and procedures, e.g., key signatures, time signatures, accidentals, rhythms, repeats, tempo, expression marks, articulation demands, diction, and/or special bowing indications.

Many variations of the day are possible. Directors could consider selecting works and/or sections of literature to sight-read based on the following areas:

- key recognition (special emphasis on certain scales or keys)

- note recognition

- rhythmic recognition (special emphasis on asymmetric meter, 6/8 time, syncopation, etc.)

- style recognition (articulation, bowing, or other similar demands)

- historical recognition

- musical structure or form recognition

- difficulty

When using this strategy, consider what assessment technique will be most appropriate to measure the results in improved performance. Both ensemble recording and playback, along with individual assessment, are notable options for consideration.

Recording Day

A frequently utilized rehearsal technique is to record and possibly play back recorded excerpts and/or entire works for individual and group assessment. Many options are possible:

- record entire works

- record special sections

- record from the front of the ensemble

- record from the rear of the ensemble

- record from within the ensemble (consider using small hand-held size recorders and place on the floor in section areas, e.g., altos, flutes, violas, etc.)

- record using several microphones each on a separate recording channel. This will allow separation of sections and areas of the ensemble for specialized analysis and playback.

- record specialty areas (solo lines, soft sections, impact sections, transitions, lyrical or technically complex areas)

- invite a specialist (recording engineer) to record — possibly for a cassette or compact disc

Listening Day

Music-listening day has a myriad of possibilities. Listening for appreciation, discrimination, and assessment, without question, is vital for all musicians. This section is only an introduction to ideas. Listening activities could include any or all of the following:

- listening to previously recorded class rehearsals or concerts

- listening to recordings of musical works recorded by other organizations

- listening to recordings of quality and poor performance for assessment purposes

- listening to recordings of similar style, structural form, historical period, composer, etc.

- listening to specific areas of the daily rehearsal — tone, intonation, blend, balance, pulse, expression, musical form, dynamics, technique, articulation, bowing, diction, etc.

- review *what* to listen for and *how* to listen — Aaron Copland's *What to Listen for in Music*

Music History and Appreciation Day

Many directors have used this strategy to reinforce the teaching of music literature from a historical perspective.

Making connections to other disciplines and cultures through a historical perspective can lead to deeper valuing, understanding, and fulfillment in music making. Therefore, the emphasis on these elements can also lead to more musical literacy, accountability, and alignment with current educational direction.[2]

Other directors have also used this strategy to address Content Standard 9 of the *National Standards for Arts Education — What Every Young American Should Know and Be Able to Do in the Arts:* Content Standard 9: *Understanding music in relation to history and culture.*[3]

Numerous presentation options include:

- presentation of the historical development of music with focus on one period of music per day, e.g., antiquity, medieval, baroque, etc. Days for this emphasis could be placed throughout the year or semester.

- students could be assigned research projects and each could provide reports on composers or other historical aspects, e.g., instruments, period structural forms, etc.

- historical perspectives could be presented addressing specific period performance practices for voice, strings, and/or instruments

- students could be presented and informed of *exemplary works of art from a variety of cultures and historical periods, thus providing a basic understanding of historical development in the arts disciplines, across the arts as a whole, and within cultures*[4]

- information could be presented which *relates various types of arts knowledge and skills within and across the arts disciplines*[5]

- the following are selected sources, references, and catalogs for instructional/historical videos, CDROMs, etc.: Gamble Musical Merchandise Catalogue 1-800-6211-4290; Videos for Music Education 1-800-519-8000; National Music Supply 1-800-768-6393; Music Technology Guide 1-800-822-6752

Student Critique Day

Student critique day works well in preparation for organizational festivals or contests in which assessment is a part of the event. Students are charged with the responsibility of evaluating the performance of the group for the day. Serving in the critique role could be section leaders, seniors, volunteers, or students selected by draw. The critique process could include the use of music scores complete with evaluation forms as well as the ensemble playing the entire program, a selection, a section, or any combination.

Guest Critique Day

The advantage of having special guests observe and critique your ensemble can be of significant benefit to you and your students. This day could include many options:

- special guests could listen to your ensemble and critique the rehearsal on video tape, cassette tape, and/or provide written comments

- some directors prefer for the critique to be given directly to the students following each selection performed

- another option would be for the special guests to work with the ensemble and possibly do master classes in a sectional format

- consider the placement of the special guests. They could listen up front beside the podium, from the audience position, or from within the ensemble.

Guest critique day could be incorporated several times a year.

Student Composer Day

Student composer day could be an extension of projects or assignments from your daily classes. The purpose of this day is to allow your students who have composed works, excerpts, or made special arrangements to have the opportunity to hear their work performed by a live ensemble. This activity connects well with Concept 4 of the *National Standards for Arts Education — What Every Young American Should Know and Be Able to Do in the Arts:*

> 4. Content Standard: Composing and arranging music within specified guidelines.[6]

To secure the success of this strategy, directors must take the time to work closely with students to see that transpositions, part writing, copying of parts, and other necessary details have been accurately completed. In order to maximize the class time and maintain classroom control, students should have the music placed in folders in advance and should avoid passing out parts during the class.

Directors should arrange to record the class for student composer listening. Consider having an individual follow-up critique with each student composer.

Guest Composer Day

Many directors have incorporated this strategy and have found this experience to be most rewarding. The primary objective of this day is to arrange for a composer to come visit and work with your ensemble on music that they have composed. Many composers will share more details concerning compositional techniques employed as well as extensive background concerning the particular work being rehearsed. The director may want to consider the following options:

- the composer could rehearse the music and provide his/her interpretation concerning various performance aspects

- the composer could provide a lecture/discussion presentation

- other classes (interdisciplinary) could be invited to observe the rehearsal and/or lecture discussion

- parents and/or other special guests could be invited to participate through observation, as well as a possible discussion

- a special question and answer time could be devoted for the last part of the class to allow students the opportunity to gain further insight into the composer's life, career, music, etc.

Student Conductor Day

Several directors have responded that the opportunity for students to share in this experience has influenced some to pursue music as a career. The purpose of this day is to provide many students the opportunity to experience rehearsing and conducting. Several options follow:

- drum majors from the school marching band who have previous experience would be excellent candidates

- consider having section leaders gain this experience

- provide the opportunity to students in music theory or appreciation class after having presented a unit on conducting

- consider having a special preparation class for interested students in which score reading, preparation, and marking, etc. would be addressed

- provide the experience for all music major prospects, especially those in their junior and/or senior years

One director indicated that this strategy works especially well on those days during the term or year in which students frequently have lower interest levels and are possibly distracted with other events. Those days seem to be preceding vacation days, e.g., fall break, Christmas break, spring break, and especially the last several days of the semester or year.

Guest Conductor Day

This strategy is encouraged of all music directors of all ensembles at all levels of ability. Unfortunately, the guest conductor day seems to be reserved for the top performing ensemble at most schools. Consider having a guest conductor for all ensembles at whatever level they may be — outstanding to remedial. Here are several suggested ideas:

- the guest conductor could be a college or university conductor

- an area composer or composer of a work being performed by your ensemble could serve well in this area, provided they also have expertise in conducting

- consider an exchange of guest conducting experiences with a fellow colleague

- invite a retired music educator to come and share. Often, outstanding retired music educators are available in your area and are an invitation away from assisting.

Other selection options include inviting the regional professional orchestra or choral conductor, the local music dealer or representative who has experience and successful background in this area, professional musicians in the area, and possibly school administrators who have served as successful music directors.

Student Soloist Day

Student soloist day works well to allow students the opportunity to perform for their peers. All students, and especially solo and ensemble candidates, as well as outstanding performers, could benefit greatly. Here are several options to consider:

- students could perform selected solos with or without live accompaniment (could work well with the *Vivace* system, if available)

- consider having selected solos performed with a large ensemble accompaniment

- have all students participate in the student soloist day. Students could perform excerpts of a solo, a complete movement, or a complete work or song.

- this day works well to have students perform All-State tryout material in front of others

- students auditioning for music entrance and scholar-ships for college serve as outstanding candidates to benefit

- consider a day to feature specialists from the entire music department of your school with all music students attending (band, orchestra, and chorus)

- possibly have local organizations sponsor scholar-ships or provide awards (to attend summer music camps, take private lessons, assist with future college tuition, purchase a new instrument or music litera-ture, etc.)

Guest Soloist Day

The objective of this day is to provide superb modeling of performance for your students. Numerous options are possible:

- the guest soloist could perform independently, with an accompanist, or with a small or large ensemble

- the guest soloist could provide his/her interpretation concerning various performance aspects (articulation, diction, historical aspects, artistic expression, etc.)

- the guest soloist could also provide a lecture/discussion presentation concerning his/her performance, about his/her instrument or vocal technique, and about the music being performed

- other classes (interdisciplinary) could be invited to observe the performance and/or lecture discussion

- parents and/or other special guests could be invited to participate through observation as well as a possible discussion

- a special question and answer time could allow students the opportunity to gain further insight into the performer's life, career, pedagogical knowledge, and music interests, etc.

Lesson Day

The purpose of hosting a lesson day is to provide a private, section, or group lesson plan. This plan does not require that the large ensemble cease to rehearse when having lesson day. There are many options for the day and include the following:

- students could rotate individually from the large ensemble for private lessons (this day is intended to include all students — not necessarily on the same day)

- sections could be designated to have a sectional for the day (not all sections would need to have lessons if space or supervision is limited)

- consider a master class approach first if starting a lesson plan for individual students. Once students have adjusted to the group lesson plan, move to small groups or duos, then to individuals.

- consider sponsorship of specialists to provide lesson day. Sponsors could include music parents, civic organizations, or local businesses.

Sectional Day

Sectional day differs from lesson day in that large groups would rehearse music being prepared for performance. The options for this day are also numerous and include some of the following:

- depending on available space, sections could all rehearse simultaneously, rotate throughout the class period, or rehearse independently

- paraprofessionals, teacher aides, parents, or volunteers could serve as supervisors of the sectionals. Rehearsal could be coordinated by the student

section leaders or possibly the supervisors, if quali-
fied.

- consider using this strategy frequently. Some directors reported that they have rotating sectionals
several times weekly and some once a week.

- consider having the sectionals videotaped, or at least
audio recorded to assess progress, to confirm
student cooperation, to reinforce supervision and
accountability of the students, or to make sure that
the time was used wisely.

Intonation Day

This day could be used to instruct students on various
aspects of performing with proper intonation. The focus
on improved pitch matching could be addressed through
the rehearsal of specific exposed areas of the music. Other
options include:

- focus on the intonation aspects of the melodic
material, unison or parallel voicing

- devote the concentration to the harmonic intonation
aspects

- incorporate varying ear-training exercises, e.g.,
interval and/or melodic dictation, sing a melody —
they play back the melody, etc.

- consider an individual assessment of each student in
regards to their ability to match pitch. Some directors have used tone generators to work on pitch
matching and measuring of the pitch matching with

a tuner or current computer-based pitch assessment program. Students could profit from this procedure if made aware of general pitch tendencies or poor notes on their instrument.

- consider repeating the above individual intonation assessment procedure several times a year. The procedure could be administered by student assistants, additional music teaching staff, hired paraprofessionals, substitute teachers, parents, and volunteers, if trained.

Research Day

Writing across the curriculum seems to be a current trend in education throughout the country. This day could be the culmination of having had students research and write reports on various fields of music topics and present their reports in class. The presentations could be in numerous formats and lengths of times depending upon the writing and research requirement. Some directors have had students write a semester paper. Select a topic from an article read in a music periodical or journal. Include the paper in the student's assessment portfolio. This day could be used for oral presentations of these reports.

Solo and Ensemble Day

Those directors interested in establishing and maintaining a year-round solo and ensemble program should consider this strategy. The purpose of this day is to allow students to rehearse solos and/or ensembles under supervision outside of the class during the regular scheduled class time. An appropriate area would have to be available as well as a plan for supervision acceptable to the school administration. Some directors have allowed students to rehearse independently as long as an audio tape and/or video tape were used during the entire rehearsal to monitor appropriate use of quality time. If this type of day were to be implemented throughout the year, students could find many opportunities to perform, which include some of the following:

- music parent meetings could feature a different ensemble or soloist for each meeting all year

- performances for school board meetings

- opportunities to perform for civic organizations

- performances for openings of businesses, special events, and festivals

- a weekly performance series for local senior citizen centers, special adult care facilities, and children's hospitals, etc.

Melody Day, Harmony Day, Rhythm Day

The objective of this day is to focus the total rehearsal on the concept of melody, harmony, or rhythm. Each rehearsal would focus on only one of the three areas each day. The options for applying this strategy are many:

- melodies could be rehearsed throughout each work being prepared for performance with concentration on uniformity, expression, musicality, etc.

- the day could focus on harmonic lines for intonation, balance, blend, expression, uniformity, etc.

- rhythm day could concentrate on rhythmic accuracy, metronomic precision, and tempo, in relation to rhythm for excerpts being prepared for performance

- each day could focus on the concept of how to perform basic melodies, harmonies, or rhythms. For example, rhythm day could include study using worksheets, rhythm reading and recognition (*Fussell Ensemble Drill Book for Band,* pages 40-41), and possibly creating a rhythmic dictionary.

For additional information, see Chapter Two, *Instrumental Music Pedagogy,* by Daniel L. Kohut, Englewood Cliffs, N.J.: Prentice-Hall, Inc., 1973.

Reading Day

This strategy day works particularly well if you know in advance that you are to have a partial class with insufficient time to take out and put up instruments. The purpose would be for students to be allowed to read an article from a periodical, journal, or book on some topic about music. Several options include:

- students could read for the period with no assessment

- students could be asked to make a brief written summary of their reading

- students could make oral reports of their work

- selected article reviews could be published in the monthly music department newsletter to parents

String Bowing Day

Proper orchestral bowing requires special attention and this strategy allows a concentrated time to provide both adequate instruction and performance time to address the topic. Several options include:

- the strings would concentrate on correct bowing styles and direction for designated excerpts from the literature being performed

- a specific day could be devoted to developing bowing styles (technique) with the aid of a specialist, e.g., on- and off-the-string *legato* bowings, on- and off-the-string *staccato* bowings, as well as special-effect bowings

For additional information, see Chapter Six, *The Dynamic Orchestra*, "Bowing Principals," by Elizabeth Green, Englewood Cliffs, N.J.: Prentice-Hall, Inc., 1987.

Woodwind and Brass Articulation Day

The objective of this day would be to have a concentrated period of time devoted to the teaching of proper technique for woodwind and brass articulation and performance style. Instructional options include:

- tongue position

- the attack syllables

- double and triple tonguing

- the basic articulations: slur, *tenuto*, *staccato*, *marcato*, and marked notes, etc.

• use of breath and/or tongue for release

For additional information, see Chapter Four, *Instrumental Music Pedagogy*, by Daniel L. Kohut, Englewood Cliffs, N.J.: Prentice-Hall, Inc., 1973.

Vocal Music Day (Tone and Diction)

The teaching strategy for this day would focus on the development of the voice as an instrument, as well as acquiring accurate diction. Topics could include any or all of the following:

• tonal quality

• breathing (proper breath support and control)

• posture

• development of range

• vocal flexibility

• vowels and resonance

• pronunciation

• enunciation

• articulation (physical action)

• vowels and consonants

• basic styles of choral diction: *legato*, *staccato*, and *marcato*

• vibrato

For further topics, see *Conducting Choral Music,* Seventh Edition, by Robert L. Garretson, Englewood Cliffs, N.J.: Prentice-Hall, Inc., 1993 and *Evoking Sound* by James Jordan, Chicago: GIA Publications, 1996.

Physics of Sound Day

Here is another day to use as a teaching strategy option for the end of school, the day before spring break, or for a break in the daily rehearsal routine. The objective of this presentation could be to introduce students to the fundamentals of how sound is produced, heard, and perceived. A special guest (physics teacher) or the music director could present the information. Topics are again numerous and could include any of the following:

- vibration (frequency and amplitude)

- the transmission of sound

- quality and timbre of sound (harmonics, envelope, noise, waveforms)

- acoustic properties of stringed, wind, and percussion instruments

- effects upon sound (speed, diffusion, reflection, refraction, diffraction, etc.)

- hearing and perception (how we hear sound — the outer, middle, and inner ear)

- hearing loss and deafness

- aural perception (physical and mental process)

For additional information, see *Introductory Musical Acoustics* by Michael J. Wagner, Third Edition, Raleigh, N.C.: Contemporary Publishing Company, 1994.

Stereo Day

Stereo Day or "Electronic Production and Reproduction of Sound Day" are extensions of the Physics of Sound Day. This day works very well as a specialty day to assist students in making wise personal choices with the purchase of sound equipment. Some ideas for topics and presentation include the following:

- invite the local stereo store specialist to come set up a display of equipment (speakers, amplifiers, microphones, CD players, video recorders, etc.) and provide a presentation

- topics could include: high fidelity versus stereophonic, monophonic sound; how to interpret the technical language; determining sound quality; storage of sound systems (analog versus digital)

Instrument Step-Up Day

The purpose of Instrument Step-Up Day is to provide instrumental students the opportunity to try out professional-line instruments in a private and/or ensemble rehearsal setting. Students could have the opportunity to ask questions, try out, and compare options of several instruments. This strategy does not necessarily have to interrupt the daily rehearsal. Interested students could rotate out of the rehearsal to another room or they could try out the instruments during rehearsal. Possibly invite interested parents to visit and hear about the benefits of better instruments and talk with the music dealer.

Music Theory Day

This day allows for concentrated teaching and experiences in music theory. Focus could be on any aspect of music theory — from aural discrimination to theoretical elements. The following represents several ideas:

- provide a sequential learning series that introduces students to the fundamentals of music. Consider the use of a program text, handouts, worksheets, or other audio-visual instructional aids.

- students could make their own dictionary using all of the musical terms (vocabulary) being used in the music they are currently performing in class

- consider relating the theory session with the music being performed with concentration on various aspects such as the key centers, structure and form, stylistic performance, and rhythmic development, etc.

For an excellent source addressing these aspects, see the following: *Band Director's Curriculum Resource* (Ready-to-Use Lessons & Worksheets for Teaching Music Theory) by Connie M. Ericksen. West Nyack, NY: Parker Publishing Co., 1998.

Endnotes

[1]Joseph Casey, *Teaching Techniques and Insights for Instrumental Music Educators* (Chicago: GIA Publications, 1993): 112.

[2]Richard Miles, ed. *Teaching Music through Performance in Band.* Volume II (Chicago: GIA Publications, 1996).

[3]Consortium of National Arts Education Associations. *National Standards for Arts Education — What Every Young American Should Know and Be Able to Do in the Arts* (Reston, VA: Music Educators National Conference, 1994).

[4]Ibid.

[5]Ibid.

[6]Ibid.

Chapter Six

Teaching and Enriching Strategies

An on-going goal of most educators is to provide opportunities for students to become independent thinkers, learners, and consumers of knowledge. The following strategies and enriching opportunities have been suggested by music teachers as ideas that have enriched their students' music education.

Instructional Enhancements

Numerous resources and instructional opportunities can be made available to assist and enhance the daily class.

Audio Resources

Students should be provided the opportunity to listen to music outside of the daily rehearsal. Some directors have established a listening center with recordings (long-play records, cassettes, and compact discs) available for student listening. Specific suggestions follow:

- audio playback units, e.g., turntable, cassette player, or compact disc player, can be made available to function with one or multiple headsets

- consider establishing a library of audio resources that students can possibly check out for a limited period for home use

- some directors require students to listen to selected music excerpts of solos and ensembles as well as large ensemble music being performed

- consider incorporating a rotation system during the daily class schedule that allows students a designated time to listen

- additional times could be made available for listening, e.g., before school, study hall, lunch period, and after school

Visual Resources

Many visual and audiovisual resources can also be made to reinforce instruction in your music class. Consider some of the following options:

- if performing literature from a particular historical style, display art work that also represents that period and provide an explanation of the visual construction and stylistic elements and possibly how the elements parallel with the music of the same period

- many location options are available for displaying art work: in the hall way, entrance to the rehearsal area, and in the rehearsal room

- include charts, graphs, and bulletin boards: fingering charts, music terminology, sight-reading procedures, outline of form and style, and historical timeline which could include the music being performed

Music Library

Most educators have numerous resources which could be made available for student use. Several directors have suggested that these resources, when shared with students, help add enrichment and encouragement to students to independently expand their knowledge of music. The following outlines several options:

- have a special rack to display books, journals, and encyclopedias on various topics that relate to your music classes, e.g., books on pedagogy, composers, music theory, history, and literature

- create a special display of music related magazines: *The Choral Journal, The Instrumentalist, Fanfare Magazine, The Music Educators Journal, Teaching Music, The Jazz Educators Journal,* etc.

- have music scores of works being performed available on display for student review and possible check-out

- start a special solo and ensemble literature library for student display, review, and check-out. One director suggested that their library was created and maintained by requiring students to contribute an older work in order to check out a new work. Music parent organizations could also be encouraged to contribute a special budgeted amount each year designated for the purchase of solo and ensemble music for student check-out.

Recording Library

The recording library serves as a source of audio recordings (long-play records, cassettes, or compact discs) that students have the opportunity to check out. The following are some suggested options to consider:

- audio recordings of great soloists

- recordings of outstanding ensembles performing similar works (literature that students may perform)

- a collection of historical recordings that reflect a sampling of the development of music, e.g., recordings that accompany *The Norton Scores,* edited by Roger Kamien, New York: W.W. Norton & Company, 1990 or *The Development of Western Music* by Marie K Stolba, Dubuque, IA: Wm. C. Brown Publishers, 1990.

- ensemble core literature recordings, e.g., *Teaching Music through Performance in Band,* (Resource Recordings for Volumes I, II, and III, Grades 2 and 3), North Texas Wind Symphony, Eugene Corporon, Conductor, Chicago: GIA Publications, 1997, 1998, 1999.

- recordings of all past concerts from your school (include program notes and other pertinent information — personnel, etc.)

- recordings of district, regional, and All-State band, orchestra, and chorus performances

Music Score Library

Some directors indicated that they have created a special music score library of full and condensed scores of all the works that are currently being performed as well as scores for the upcoming concert. Several options follow:

- students could check out scores for review

- consider having the section leaders use scores for sectionals and/or for any student's use when listening to recordings of rehearsals and/or sectionals

- scores could be available for review when listening to works in the audio resources library

- provide rehearsal scores for student review that have been marked indicating special performance concerns, e.g., problem areas, special sections of melodic emphasis, tempo modifications or inter-pretations, outlined form and structure, etc.

Computer-Assisted Resources

There are numerous ways to provide computer-assisted resources. Several directors have indicated that they received special instructional grants to establish a computer lab. Here are several options to consider as part of your computer lab:

- computer complete with MIDI capabilities

- software for music writing and arranging

- software for intonation assessment

- software for marching band drill design

- the new *Vivace* solo accompanying system (available from Coda Music Technologies)

- software for jazz improvisation development

- keyboards for ear training and piano technique development

- music dictionaries and encyclopedias on CDROM

- Internet access with a posted listing of special music related addresses

Composition Lab

The composition lab could take many forms. The lab could be in a special corner of the ensemble rehearsal room or in a separate room. Include the following:

- a table, keyboard, computer with composition writing software, manuscript paper, and pencils, etc.

- special books on theory, arranging, and composing

Improvisation Lab

Many sources are available which could serve as helpful aids for developing improvisation technique. Recordings, books, and computer-assisted software could be placed in a special area or special room. An excellent computer program entitled *Band In A Box,* available from Peter Gannon (PG Music Inc., Buffalo, NY), works especially well to help develop technique and fluency with improvisation.

Rhythm Lab

A special lab area designated for rhythmic development can provide an additional opportunity for students to gain further music literacy skills. The lab could contain many sources. Here are some suggested ideas:

- provide books, articles, and journals on rhythmic development

- make available a cassette recorder/playback for use with recording and listening to programmed rhythmic development studies

- include a metronome(s) for student use

- consider providing sources regarding such aspects as tempo and pulse, subdivision and meter

- include teaching aids and visual system charts that assist students with counting, vocalization, and syllables

- create, and have available for use, a rhythm dictionary — visual and/or sound (a source that defines all aspects of rhythm and possibly displays visual rhythmic examples with recorded excerpts)

- some excellent sources: *Rhythm Reading* by Daniel Kazez, Second Edition, New York: W.W. Norton & Co., 1997 (a student program learning text) and an interactive computer software program entitled *Practica Musica* available from Arsnova

Teacher Resource Guides

Numerous resources are available that can assist music directors in selecting music, developing units for instruction, creating lesson plans, and providing detailed information on composers and other literature aspects. The following is a sampling:

- *Blueprint for Band* by Robert J. Garofalo, Ft. Lauderdale, FL: Meredith Music Publications, 1983.

- *Guides to Band Masterworks* by Robert J. Garofalo, Volumes I & II, Ft. Lauderdale, FL: Meredith Music Publications, 1992.

- *Instructional Designs for Middle/Junior High School Band* by Robert J. Garofalo, Volumes I & II, Ft. Lauderdale, FL: Meredith Music Publications, 1995.

- *Listening Guides for Band Musicians* by Roland Stycos, Portland, MA: J. Weston Walch Publisher, 1991.

- *Music in the Middle/Junior High School: Syllabus/Handbook* by The University of the State of New York, The State Education Department, Bureau of Curriculum

Development, Albany, NY: New York State Education Department.

- *Teaching Musicianship in the High School Band* by Joseph A. Labuta, Revised Version, Ft. Lauderdale, FL: Meredith Music Publications, 1998.

- *Teaching Music through Performance in Band,* edited by Richard Miles, Volumes I, II, & III, Chicago, IL: GIA Publications, 1996, 1998, 1999.

- *Teaching Techniques and Insights* by Joseph L. Casey, Chicago, IL: GIA Publications, 1993.

Field Trips

If used as an academic extension of the class, field trips could assist greatly with reinforcing learning. Music ensemble directors have used this enrichment strategy for years. Here are several ideas that have been suggested:

- take the ensemble members to hear a professional level choir, orchestra, or band. Prepare in advance for the visit. Review the selections to be performed and post program notes in addition to discussing proper listening guidelines and etiquette.

- perform an exchange concert with another school with directors rotating the conducting.

- visit an art museum with the intent of making transfers of visual art and historical and stylistic development to the music currently being performed by your ensemble

- visit a local university school of music and set up special master classes and have a presentation provided to your students on music career options

- participate in a music assessment event in which your ensemble performs, followed by a hands-on clinic

- if available in your area, visit a music manufacturing company and explore the details of the industry and the intricacies of creating musical instruments, e.g., piano, woodwind, brass, or percussion factory

Special Workshops

As an addition to your daily class, organize a series of workshops for special interest areas and invite guests to share. The following is a sampling of suggested ideas:

- a seminar on voice pedagogy, diction, or special breathing development

- a seminar on double reed making or single reed curing and adjustment

- a series of special seminars on how to do your own instrument repair (springs, corks, pads, etc.), proper cleaning and daily maintenance, and possibly piano tuning

- a seminar on basic conducting technique and preparation of drum major tryouts for the marching band

- have a series of lessons on how to use a music notation software program such as *Finale*

- a seminar hosted by professional musicians and/or university faculty on preparing for All-State band, orchestra, or chorus tryouts

Concert and Lecture Series

This area is often overlooked and worthy of considering. Schedule a year-long concert and lecture series for your school and music program. Acquire sponsorship from civic organizations, the local school board, or local and regional arts councils for the concerts. The series could be during and/or after school. Here are several ideas for artists:

- professional musicians — soloists

- guest ensembles, e.g., civic choir; local orchestra; community band, service band, orchestra, or choir; local jazz combo; or ensembles

- guest conductors

- shared or joint concerts with other school groups

- exchange concerts with other school groups

- musicologists to present aspects of world music

- guests to present information concerning folk music and/or folk instruments

Scheduling Within the Class

Several ideas have been addressed in the "Daily Teaching Strategies" section previously presented. Many of those ideas include students having the opportunity to simultaneously participate in enrichment activities while the ensemble continues to rehearse. Those ideas include: sectionals, master classes, solo and ensemble rehearsal, shared members between two music classes (e.g., band/orchestra/chorus), and special learning enrichment labs.

Chapter Seven

Assessment of Music Performance

"A *grade* can be regarded only as an inadequate report of an inaccurate judgment by a biased and variable judge of the extent to which a student has attained an undefined level of mastery of an unknown proportion of an indefinite amount of material."

— *Punished by Rewards*, A. Kohn

Gathering Information

Assessment involves gathering information about the learning process. Student assessment refers to some form of direct examination of student performance in tasks that are considered significant.[1] According to Elliot Eisner, "performance assessment is one of the 'hot topics' on the agenda of education reform."[2] "As education in America has passed from teacher-driven recitation to government-driven accountability, the role of formal assessment has grown."[3] Eisner suggests that "performance assessment affords us, in principle, an opportunity to develop ways of revealing the distinctive features of individual students."[4] Viewed as an active part of the music instruction process, assessment has the potential not only to provide teacher feedback for music students, but also to provide opportunities for music students to participate, to give on-going feedback on their own individual and ensemble music knowledge and skill development. Assessment — an essential part of the teaching/learning process in a music performance setting — is a joint responsibility of both music teachers and music students.[5]

Assessment, Evaluation, and Music Teachers

Music teachers must make decisions about what assessment strategies they will use to gather information about individual student and group learning in performance settings. Additionally, these same music teachers must decide how they will use the information. In general, the term **assessment** refers to the means and tools — the strategies — used to gather information about students and their achievements. The term **evaluation** refers to the judgments and decisions made about students and their work as a result of assessment.[6] Finding meaningful and manageable ways to assess and evaluate the progress of the many students of different ages and performance levels often found in the same ensemble is important.

Periodic playing/singing tests, written tests covering the theoretical and historical elements of music, attendance, and participation have all held places in the evaluation of students in ensembles for decades.[7] However, the *National Standards for Music Education* may provide an expanded foundation for student assessment in performing groups.

National Standards for Music Education
(1994)

Creating and Performing
- Singing, alone and with others, a varied repertoire of music
- Performing on instruments alone and with others, a varied repertoire of music
- Reading and notating music
- Improvising melodies, variations, and accompaniments
- Composing and arranging music within specified guidelines

Perceiving and Analyzing
- Listening to, analyzing, and describing music
- Evaluating music and music performances

Understanding Relationships
- Understanding relationships among music, history, and culture
- Understanding relationships among music, the other arts, and disciplines outside the arts[8]

James Austin suggests that "the standards clearly distinguish music instruction from status-quo teaching practices that are narrow in scope or emphasize activity without insight."[9] By replacing the words *instruction* and *teaching* with *assessment* in the preceding sentence, the National Standards may provide assessment opportunities that will also enhance (not replace) traditional assessment practices. Austin points out that with the exception of the standard addressing curricular integration, the National Standards for Music Education may be viewed as a "repackaging" of comprehensive musicianship which he defines as "performance with understanding."[10]

Assessing Performance with Understanding

Both the National Standards and comprehensive musicianship principles affirm the need for music students to acquire both music knowledge (understanding) and skills matters, and suggest that these aspects of musical learning can and should be assessed in a variety of ways. The following assessment strategies, reported to be in use by music teachers across the country, focus on student involvement in an assessment process that includes creating and performing, perceiving and analyzing, and understanding relationships. Music teachers are encouraged to carefully consider the intended purpose of any assessment procedure before implementation.

Student Self-Critiques
Student Peer Critiques
Student Rehearsal Critiques
Student Performance Critiques

Seeing and/or hearing ourselves as others see or hear us is the basis for this assessment technique. The focus is on students' (individual or group) assessment/evaluation of their own performances or the performances of others. Student response opportunities have ranged from rating performances using specific criteria to providing oral/ written comments appropriate to the purpose of the assessment task.

Student Individual Performance Checklists

Similar to the previous student critique techniques, the focus here is on student perception and analysis of individual performance using a *checklist* approach. Checklists have ranged from execution techniques (hand position, breath control, embouchure/bow, articulation, diction, vibrato) to overall performance categories of tone, intonation, rhythmic accuracy, and musicianship.

Student Section Progress Charts

The focus here is on section performance within the context of a larger ensemble. Depending on the purpose of the assessment task, students have provided feedback on their own section or other sections within their own or other ensembles.

Student Attitude Surveys

This assessment strategy is based on the idea that if you want to know how students feel about something, you ask them. Specific applications have included student attitudes about music performances, music selection, music preferences, and performance preferences.

Student Group Discussions

Teachers have been described as shapers of the environment, stimulators, motivators, guides, consultants, and resources.[11] Music teachers, using appropriate questioning techniques, have reported that student decision-making and discussion within the context of a music rehearsal has become an important part of their regular rehearsal activity. These techniques are giving students the opportunity to demonstrate musical understanding in new ways.

Student Creative Projects/Portfolios

Traditional assessment techniques have focused heavily on student performance. Student creative projects and portfolios have provided opportunities for students to document not only performance competency (individual performance tapes, solo/ensemble participation), but also to include reports on composers, compositions being performed, listening projects, and composition assignments. The portfolio in particular has become an important tool for documenting student learning in music over a period of time.

Endnotes

[1]Miles, R.(Ed.). *Teaching Music through Performance in Band,* Chicago: G.I.A. Publications, p. 27.

[2]Elliot W. Eisner, "The Uses and Limits of Performance Assessment," Phi Delta Kappan, May, 1999, p. 658.

[3]Robert Stake, "The Goods on American Education," Ibid, p. 669.

[4]Eisner, p. 660.

[5]Miles, p. 27.

[6]Ibid., p. 28.

[7]David Scott, "Tiered Evaluation in Large Ensemble Settings," *Music Educators Journal,* November, 1998, p. 17.

[8]James R. Austin, "Comprehensive Musicianship Research: Implications for Addressing the National Standards in Music Ensemble Classes," *Update: Applications of Research in Music Education,* Fall-Winter, 1998, p. 26.

[9]Ibid., p. 25.

[10]Ibid.

[11]Eisner, p. 658.

Chapter Eight

Using Time Wisely

Time-Saving Strategies

The following list of strategies is intended to assist in the organization and administration of class duties and activities, thus allowing fewer distractions and possibly providing more efficient use of rehearsal time.

Several of the following ideas come from a wonderful presentation that was made at the 56th MENC National Biennial In-Service in Phoenix, Arizona. The special session, "Quality Time Management in the Band Room," was presented by Dr. Barbara Payne of the University of Hawaii–Manoa.

- List the musical selections to be rehearsed in advance. Place the listing on a bulletin board (posted in the entrance to the rehearsal room) and on the chalkboard in the rehearsal room.

- Use the chalkboard or the handout mentioned above for all announcements. Include information concerning upcoming events and activities. Reminders addressing fundraising aspects can save time and can serve as an additional reinforcement.

- Make instrument or voice part assignments, leadership assignments, and *especially* percussion assignments, in advance of the first rehearsal. Pass out and post the assignments for continued reference throughout the semester.

- Create a "Discipline Plan." The following eight steps, presented by Jana Fallin, James Murphy, David Royce, and Chris Richmond at the 55th MENC National Biennial In-Service Conference in Kansas City, Missouri, serve as an excellent reference in establishing this strategy:

  1. Learn your school's discipline policy.

  2. Establish rules for your classroom.

     - short and positive

     - five to six in number

  3. Determine positive reinforcement.

     - may or may not be clearly stated

     - don't reinforce inappropriate behavior

  4. Determine consequences.

     - make the punishment fit the crime

     - include a "severe clause"

5. Present the plan to your administrator.

6. Communicate the plan to parents.

7. Make it visible in the classroom.

8. Enforce it from *Day One*.

• Establish and post "Rehearsal Expectations" with your "Discipline Plan," e.g., time to enter classroom, how to obtain music, when to have a seat, procedures for music rehearsal readiness (pencils, reeds, strings, instrument repairs, etc.) cutoffs, and questions.

• Make sure that all measures are numbered in each selection for quick rehearsal reference. Consider this strategy as an option that will likely save time and numerous distractions because of student error in quickly and accurately locating the rehearsal concern.

• If there are known printing errors in the music, make the corrections on the parts in advance or pass out the errata and have students make the corrections.

• Notate interpretation marks on the individual parts prior to distribution to students. This will save time, especially if there are volume and/or articulation changes or clarifications. Consider using different colors, e.g., red, blue, yellow.

• Require all students to have and use pencils in every rehearsal. Eliminating the necessity to repeat corrections and instructions can save a great deal of time.

- Utilize students or parents to serve in varying administrative and assisting roles. In addition to saving time, this organizational strategy shares the ownership of the music program and helps to eliminate many distractions during class. Here are several specific roles:

  Music Librarian (responsible for all aspects of music issuing, maintenance, collection, and filing)

  Class Manager (assists with the classroom set-up and take-down, makes sure that any special instructional needs are available and set up, e.g., audio recorder with mikes, overhead projector, stereo, VCR)

  Equipment and Supplies Manager (handles the distribution and sale of reeds, valve oil, etc.; manages the check-out of school instruments; and coordinates all aspects of fundraising, including the collection of money; etc.)

  Attendance and Role Monitor (responsible for taking and reporting the daily class attendance)

  Telephone and Visitor Monitor (answers the telephone and takes messages as well as meets and greets visitors, e.g., parents, fund-raiser sales personnel, and music dealer representatives)

  Uniform Manager (responsible for issuing, repairing, cleaning, and maintaining inventory of the uniforms, concert choir robes, etc. for performances)

Secretary (parent volunteer(s) could serve several of the above roles as well as help prepare daily handouts, correspondence, trip schedules, concert programs, and assist with area monitoring)

- Consider having music stands set up and taken down for each rehearsal. Store the stands in racks. This task will allow the classroom to be more easily cleaned and ensures that each ensemble sets up without any extra seating or placement restraints.

- Another strategy to improve classroom organization is to set up and take down chairs for each ensemble and place the chairs in special chair storage racks. Some directors have reported that instead of taking down chairs for each class, they set up for the first class and take down the final class of the day. This procedure still allows for improved cleaning and maintenance of the classroom.

- All music classrooms seem to need more trash cans. Place one trash can in the entrance, one in all practice and storage rooms, and especially one in all corners of the rehearsal room. This can help to eliminate excessive, distractive, and longer student trips to discard trash, e.g., chewing gum, broken reeds, drum sticks, etc.

- Store all instruments in lockers. Although storing instruments takes time (to put up and take out), more time is likely saved in eliminating security issues, maintaining classroom neatness, and cleaning.

- Another idea to help eliminate unnecessary distractions during the daily classes is to utilize bookshelves to store all carry-in items. Bookshelves should be located at the entrance to the rehearsal room. This strategy helps students avoid having items stored under and around their seating, thus helping to eliminate tripping and potential distractions with students doing work from other classes, e.g., writing and passing notes, etc.

- Have students store their music in a special folder rack. This procedure will make it easier for distribution and collection of music and will help insure that folders are available when students are out of class and share music folders.

- Organize a special storage area for all percussion equipment and accessories to be used in daily rehearsals. Consider making *bold, visible labels* to help students be organized with the storage and assign a percussion manager for each class to see that all equipment is returned and accounted for. Avoid simply placing accessories randomly in a cabinet.

- One director suggested that all percussionists should be assigned a special area for their *own individual performance space.* The space should be clearly marked and separated from others. Percussionists would not travel out of their space during the class unless rotating spaces for instrumentation changes, e.g., snare to bass drum, bass drum to mallets, mallets to timpani. This suggestion was made to assist with behavior control, especially with younger age students who are often tempted with other non-musical activities. Each space should be clearly separated from all others.

- Establish a system for dealing with instruments that need repair. Create a special instrument "Repair Form" or "String Tag" for student use. The form or tag could be filled out by the student who would identify the problem, e.g., location such as the Bb key or water key cork. In order to avoid class distractions, have the students fill out the form and place it in the case or attach the tag and put the instrument in your office before or after class. The instrument could then be repaired between classes or sent to the instrument repair shop. An automatic system will potentially save numerous minutes of having to address such problems during prime rehearsal time.

The following series of Time Comparison Charts may assist in identifying the impact of "poor time management" and distractions in rehearsals. Chart 1 identifies the various daily class length options and provides the total yearly minutes of instruction available based on the nationwide average of 180 instructional days. Chart 2 provides information for rotating day schedules and lists the minutes of rehearsal available for the year. Note that Chart 2 is based on a total of 90 instructional days. Charts 3 and 4 provide a comparison of the minutes of instruction available and the impact of the daily and *yearly loss of rehearsal time due to poor time management and/or distractions.* How much loss of rehearsal time is acceptable? The charts are quite revealing and have significant implications as to the importance of our daily management of time.

Using Time Wisely
Chart 1
Yearly Minutes of Instruction Available
Based on Daily Length of Classes

Daily Class Length	Total Minutes of Yearly Class Time
45 minutes	8,100 minutes
50	9,000
55	9,900
60	10,800
65	11,700
70	12,600
75	13,500
80	14,400
85	15,300
90	16,200
120	21,600

Using Time Wisely
Chart 2
Yearly Minutes of Instruction Available
Based on "Rotating" Schedule Classes
(every other day — "A/B")

Daily Class Length	Total Minutes of Yearly Class Time
80 minutes	7,200 minutes
85	7,650
90	8,100
95	8,500
100	9,000
105	9,450
110	9,900
115	10,350
120	10,800

Using Time Wisely
Chart 3

Yearly "Minutes" and "Days" of Instruction Lost
Due to Poor Classroom Management and/or Distractions

Daily Loss of Class Time	Yearly Loss of Class Time (in 180 Days)	45	50	Yearly Loss of Rehearsals "Daily Length of Classes"				
				55	60	65	70	75
5 minutes	900 minutes	20	18	16.4	15	13.8	12.9	12
10	1,800	40	36	32.7	30	27.7	25.7	24
15	2,700	60	54	49.0	45	41.5	38.6	36
20	3,600	80	72	65.5	60	55.3	51.4	48

Daily Loss of Class Time	Yearly Loss of Class Time (in 180 Days)	80	85	Yearly Loss of Rehearsals "Daily Length of Classes"				
				90	95	100	110	120
5 minutes	900 minutes	11.2	10.6	10	9.5	9	8.2	7.5
10	1,800	22.5	21.2	20	18.9	18	16.4	15.0
15	2,700	33.7	31.8	30	28.4	27	24.5	22.5
20	3,600	45.0	42.4	40	37.9	36	32.7	30.0

Using Time Wisely
Chart 4

Yearly "Minutes" and "Days" of Instruction Lost
Due to Poor Classroom Management and/or Distractions

Daily Loss of Class Time	Yearly Loss of Class Time (in 90 Days)	Yearly Loss of Rehearsals "Rotating Class Schedules"						
		80 (A/B)	85 (A/B)	90 (A/B)	95 (A/B)	100 (A/B)	110 (A/B)	120 (A/B)
5 minutes	450 minutes	5.7	5.3	5	4.7	4.5	4.1	3.8
10	900	11.3	10.6	10	9.5	9.0	8.2	7.5
15	1,350	16.9	15.9	15	14.2	13.5	12.2	11.3
20	1,800	22.5	21.2	20	18.9	18.0	16.4	15.0

Chapter Nine

Creating Variety in Performances

Performing music should be the culmination of having used quality music literature to teach about the music, through the music, while preparing the music. All too often, the planning and importance of the performance is overlooked or underestimated. There is great potential for continued delivery of musical ideas and concepts through performing.

The following strategies addressing performance variety are intended to enhance the instruction, delivery style, and enjoyment of music making and are not intended in any way to substitute for the teaching of comprehensive musicianship and the use of quality music of artistic merit. These strategies are based, in part, on an article featured in *Fanfare* magazine, March, 1994 issue, and are used with permission. Also included are additional ideas exchanged in a special graduate continuing

education class sponsored by VanderCook College of
Music, Chicago, Illinois, in the fall of 1998.

> Creative concert programming requires
> advanced planning, unique ideas, and most
> importantly, variety. Too often music directors
> develop a habit of using the same style of selec-
> tions, the same length, location, and appear-
> ance for all our concerts. Consequently, the
> audience expects the same concert program
> every time. Only the tunes have changed. When
> programming creatively, involve visual and
> aural variety and the response from our patrons
> will be fresh, new, and different. In addition,
> our concerts will be enjoyed and appreciated
> more and will, most likely, attract a larger
> audience.[1]

The following is a listing of creative programming ideas
to use to establish variety.

Creative Concerts

- A *Theme Concert* works well to emphasize music
  programmed to address a special subject or topic.
  The entire concert could be dedicated to programming music of a similar style: Baroque, Classical,
  Romantic, Contemporary, "classical pops," Broad-
  way selections, marches (international, American,
  etc.), holiday. Several more specific theme concert
  ideas follow.

- Host a specific *Composition Style Concert,* one concert which features composition styles such as marches, overtures, waltzes, concertos, symphonies, etc.

- Consider having a *Historical Style Concert* that emphasizes a specific period of music history. This is a particularly useful tool if you are using a multi-year *historical cyclic approach* to teaching music education in your performing arts class. This could be a great *extension* of the classroom experience to share with parents and friends.

- A winner in most communities, host a *Veterans' Honor Concert.* Include the school ROTC program, local or regional National Guard, local veterans' organizations, e.g., VFW, American Legion, local or regional military base personnel, and possible military music organizations.

- Host a *Multi-Cultural Concert.* The concert could focus on music from around the world, Oriental, Latin American, European, African, etc. Special information such as the varying stylistic differences, construction, as well as the instrumentation and voicing, could be presented.

- Consider featuring the music of one composer. The *All One Composer Concert* could include many possibilities. Examples include: the music of Bernstein, Copland, Wagner, Beethoven, or Bach.

- A special end of the year idea is to hold a *Variety Highlights* or *Yearbook Concert.* The objective of this concert would be to have the performing groups feature the *best* selections of the year. Consider using this concert for special recognition of students, parents, and administrators.

- Consider hosting a special *Benefit Concert.* Admission could be a contribution of canned food for the needy, used eyeglasses for an international eye assistance organization such as the Lions Club, used winter coats for distribution by the local Salvation Army or Goodwill Industries organizations.

- A special *Madrigal Dinner/Concert* could feature historically appropriate activities and costumes. Many choral programs have successfully utilized this idea as a banquet/concert and have generated additional revenue for their program.

- Host an *Exchange Concert.* Frequently, we only consider performing alone at our own school. Consider joining efforts with other colleagues from other schools. Exchange performing locations, possibly perform jointly at both locations. One director indicated that they worked out, through their city council and board of education, the opportunity to participate in an exchange trip with another band from an international *sister city* to do a series of *exchange concerts.*

- *Showcase Many Groups on One Concert.* Consider a performance *in the round,* maybe held in the cafeteria or gymnasium — "Boston Pops" style. Each group would be set up and would rotate performing. A small stage in a central location could be for transition features between the main groups — enabling students who double in groups to move to the other setup. This aspect is very important in avoiding *dead time*. Examples of performing groups: Elementary, Middle School, High School Band, Orchestra, and Chorus. Also, Jazz Bands, Show Choirs, Strolling Strings, as well as several high school performing groups could participate on the same program.

- Seek opportunities to *Perform for Different Audiences at Different Locations*. Consider taking advantage of performing for local meetings, e.g., Chamber of Commerce, town meetings, local and regional fairs, Jaycees. You may want to consider volunteering to perform for your school *graduation*. Directors often consider this a pain, yet it may be the largest audience and the most exposure of your music program that you will receive in a concert setting. Most importantly, you can count on your *administrators* attending this event! Also, seek opportunities to perform concerts at local, state, and national festivals and music conventions. Create a concert tour to area elementary and middle schools featuring a music appreciation approach or an introduction to the various instruments or voices. Do not discard the opportunity to perform for small groups and classes — most often these audiences are very attentive and find the experience educationally rewarding.

Concert Enhancements

- Feature a *Guest Artist* (Soloist). Every concert should feature a soloist. Too often we directors think this is not possible because we cannot afford "Doc Severinsen" or "Wynton Marsalis" to come solo with our group. Consider featuring your own students with solos they may have prepared for Solo and Ensemble Contest. Other possibilities include an area music teacher who is a particularly gifted musician, your colleague who is the choral, band, or orchestra director, a local piano teacher, and regional or state university professors. Most of these persons seek opportunities to perform and are likely an invitation away from sharing. Do not let the unfamiliarity of the music literature for solos dampen your creative programming. There are many works of varying difficulty levels available. Plan and research your possibilities. Is this area worthy of a financial investment? Many of us do not hesitate to spend a thousand dollars on a new set of flags to use for 30 seconds of our marching band closer, or $500 to $2,500 for a marching drill, or specially arranged music for our show choir. Not that the above appropriations are wrong, but equal or greater financial investment in our concert program is a good way to establish a good balance in our overall music program.

• Involve a *Guest Conductor(s)*. Inviting a guest conductor to work with your ensemble and to provide a special clinic is a wonderful way to enhance the musical awareness and growth of your group. Consider inviting the retired music director in your town to conduct a selection. Perhaps you could involve an area music director, a university director, your principal, superintendent, or school board chairman. How about your football or basketball coach conducting *The Stars and Stripes Forever* or the school fight song or alma mater, or some other selection your ensemble can perform on auto pilot?

• Provide the opportunity for *Students to Conduct* on the program. Consider having a special preparation class for interested students in which score reading, preparation, marking, and rehearsing, etc. would be addressed. Several directors have responded that the opportunity for students to share in this experience has influenced some to pursue music as a career.

• Feature *Small Ensembles*. This area is too often over-looked. Consider featuring your outstanding soloists and ensembles as a part of every concert. This may include percussion ensemble, brass choir, guitar, piano, woodwind, string, or vocal ensembles or small combos. What a great way to establish and maintain a year-around solo and ensemble program rather than the more traditional two-month contest-oriented approach.

• *Commission and Premier a New Composition.* When considering who to commission to compose a piece for your ensemble to perform, look to more than the obvious, well-known composers. Also, consider lesser-known individuals who would welcome the opportunity to have their composition performed publicly. All of us know someone like this but seldom consider asking them to write for our group. Possible candidates may be arrangers for marching band and/or church music, college professors, and composition majors at local universities.

- *Premier Student Compositions.* Do you have a student particularly talented in this area? Create a great incentive for your music theory class by highlighting the top arrangement or original composition in your next concert. Promote it in your local newspaper and you will reward the outstanding student as well as inform the community of your concert in an interesting and unique manner.

- Feature *Special Musical Groups* as the audience enters and exits the main performance area. These groups may consist of the elementary and/or middle school band, orchestra, chorus, small ensembles, high school jazz groups or combos, choral ensembles, and piano soloists, etc. Spotlight the performance area in the lobby using special staging and decoration, as these groups perform prior to and following the main program. Involving more students in the concert often results in better attendance.

- Feature an *Alumni Ensemble.* Most directors have former students who have gone on to continue performing. Invite these outstanding musicians to get together and prepare a feature for your concert. Using alumni students in this way presents your current students with appropriate role models and may encourage them to continue using their talent after high school.

- Consider featuring a *Parent/Child Performance.* Do you have a parent of an ensemble member who is also an outstanding musician? Consider a feature selection focusing on the combined talents of parent and child. Perhaps an entire family could be featured.

- Involve *Other Student Groups* to perform on the concert. Many schools have an outstanding cheerleader squad, drill team, dance team, and/or auxiliary unit. Consider having a special time for one or several to perform. These performances create an enjoyable diversion from stage changes and other transitions in your concert program as well as provide for more student ownership of the concert.

- Include a *Sing-Along* portion on the program. This idea could be challenging if not thoroughly planned and the selection to sing-along carefully selected. Special feature concerts generally work well for this idea. Consider carols for a holiday concert, possibly *The Star Spangled Banner* as an opening to a Veteran's Day Concert, or the school alma mater, if hosting an alumni concert.

- Invite *Special Guests to Join the Ensemble* for one selection. This is a great time to invite upcoming middle school students to join the ensemble on one selection. Consider the many options for potential guests. How about inviting school faculty, staff, or administrative members or parents, local musicians, or guest performers who also play an instrument or sing?

- For concert programming variety, one director recommended having *All Members of the Ensemble Play Percussion Instruments* on one selection. This selection could be used to teach percussion instrumentation, part writing, and the study of rhythm, etc.

- Consider *Varying the Time of Day* for your concerts. Feature a *Breakfast Concert* serving cinnamon rolls and coffee; a *Coffee Concert* or *Coffee House Concert* where small groups could be featured in a more informal setting; a *Bach's Lunch Concert;* an *Informal Evening-Out Concert* where the "Boston Pops" style setting could feature "classical pops" music with guests sitting at tables where popcorn could be served in brown paper bags with the program printed on the bag.

- *Vary the Days of the Week* when concerts are held. Some potential attendees (especially administrators and civic leaders) could have year-long conflicts with attending your programs if you only have concerts on the same *Thursday* night. Consider rotating the most desirable days.

- Have a *Silent Auction to Select Someone to Conduct the Ensemble*. Use this fundraising idea to provide the opportunity for someone to conduct a work previously rehearsed to be performed on *auto pilot* by your group. Present the selected conductor with a souvenir baton and make arrangements to have photographs taken of him/her conducting. Many local papers look for photograph features like this one — especially if the candidate is a high profile member of the community, etc.

- One director recommended having a *Wishing Well for Special Music Requests* for upcoming concerts. The intent would be to encourage audience participation, idea exchanges, and direct input from those attending concerts. Selected works recommended from the *Wishing Well* music would then be performed by the small ensemble or feature group musicians employed as diversions for stage changes, etc.

• *Spotlight Student Art Works.* Invite the high school, middle school, or elementary schools to exhibit their art works in the lobby prior to the concert. This is a great way to involve more students and parents and to share the spotlight with others.

• Utilize *Attractive Concert Programs and Tickets.* Professional looking programs go a long way toward enhancing the image of your ensemble and can help promote your values of excellence. Keep in mind, people often *hear what they see.* Also, advanced ticket distribution, whether sold or complimentary, assists with the advertisement and community awareness of your programs. Consider creating a listing of special guests (administrators and community leaders) who receive complimentary tickets for all concerts. One great idea of *custom program-making* involves having each student's picture taken with a digital camera and having the individual student picture merged into a frame on the front cover of 15-20 concert programs per each student. Thus, custom individualized student pictures with programs would be available and placed on tables in the lobby for each of the students' invited family and special friends. The same idea could be transferred to create *custom tickets.* Consider the significance of recruiting and image-making with the use of your concert programs and tickets.

- Utilize *Program Notes.* You can enhance your performance, provide the audience information concerning the music being performed, inform all concerning special performers, and help establish a better understanding of your overall concert program with the use of program notes. Consider having students or parents prepare the program notes for inclusion in the concert program. You may want to include students' reactions to the programming, individual composer's thoughts concerning a specific work, or provide the historical setting and background. These notes may also be presented by way of multi-media. Instead of printing them in the concert program, have them projected on a large screen or on an adjacent wall (using the overhead or slide projector). Also, consider sending the program notes in the mail in advance of the concert to assist with recruiting attendees and informing administrators of your upcoming program.

- Involve *Guest or Student Announcers/Narrators.* This is a great way to again share the spotlight with special friends. Students from the ensemble could be selected to assist. Consider inviting the school *Speech and Debate Team* or *Drama Club,* etc. to contribute in this area. Highlight the announcement area. And if doing a theme concert, student or guest announcers could dress to fit the theme and possibly *act out* some portion of the presentation (Renaissance Concert/ Renaissance Dress and Speech).

- *Display Pictures and Scrapbooks* from recent and past years regarding the performing ensemble. Set up a special display in the front lobby. This idea can attract alumni, parents, and community members to rekindle fond memories with the display of photos and pertinent memorabilia. Create a meaningful night for these important individuals and remind current students of their rich heritage.

- *Involve Appropriate Humor.* Although somewhat difficult to accomplish and possibly distracting to some pursuits, well-used humor can enhance a smooth programming flow and provide emotional relief for the audience. Humor is not intended to distract from the presentation of great music, but rather to add variety. For example, Santa or an elf could make an appearance at your Holiday Concert. Comic skits also work well and create an enjoyable diversion during a stage change or transition, e.g., from concert to jazz band or concert band to symphony orchestra or concert choir.

Visual and Aural Enhancement

- *Variety is Essential — Music and Visual.* Remember that musical variety is created by varying the selections. Consider the musical style, tempo, keys, texture, volume contrast, woodwind, brass, and percussion exposure. Also, remember the need for visual variety. Consider the use of staging, color, placement of special features, use of props, risers, and backdrops. *Make your concert a production.*

- *Plan All Stage Changes.* Remember that all side act numbers, small ensemble performance, soloists, kaleidoscope group performances, etc., all require stop time and stage changes. Avoid at all costs the typical college *recital syndrome* (perform one work, leave stage — bring out one stand, return; perform next piece, leave stage — move piano, return; next piece, leave stage — set up four chairs, bring out four stands, move harpsichord, etc.). This delay process can be deadly to maintaining interest. Do all you can to avoid delays by being creative and inserting the necessary variety. Think through and make all arrangements for changes in advance. Try to consider all aspects of your performance and make provision for every part. For example, assign a stage manager, incorporate a stage crew, curtain puller, recruit ushers and ticket takers, etc. Make sure they know what their individual jobs entail, how they are expected to dress, and the importance of their position in making the whole concert run smoothly.

- *Utilize Visual Enhancement.* The use of special lighting and color can be helpful in setting and enhancing the mood of your program. Consider the use of special lighting changes, highlights, and effects to add variety. The use of backdrops can also make a significant contribution. If your school produces plays, music theater shows or something similar, you may be able to incorporate some of the props and backdrops into your program. Other special effects worthy of consideration are slides, a background screen with slides and special color changes, snow, props, smoke, etc. Keep in mind the effectiveness of a special decor to enhance the theme of your concert. A holiday concert program is especially conducive for enhancement by decor, such as the use of greenery, floral plants, risers covered in metallic mylar, Christmas lights, and artificial candles, etc.

Maintain the Highest Performance Standards Involving Quality Music of Artistic Merit

* Finally, perhaps the most important aspect to keep in mind is that none of these ideas can ever take the place of high performance standards incorporating the performance of *quality music of artistic merit.* If your performance is not excellent, a cosmetic cover-up will never be sufficient substitution. On the other hand, when great literature and high performance standards are at the core of your program, creative performing strategies can greatly enhance your overall effect and provide additional exposure and enjoyment for your students.

Endnote

¹Richard Miles, "Creative Ideas for Programming Concerts," *Fanfare,* Volume 7, Issue 1, March 1994, p. 1, 11.

Closure:

Looking Forward

When you're through *changing,*
you're *through.*
— *Bruce Barton*

According to June Hinkley, President of MENC: The National Association for Music Education:

> As we look to the future, we know that many things will and should change. It is important that we be leaders, not followers, in charting that change. It is equally important to determine, amid the climate of change, those things that are essential to the music education process...

The challenge to ***just teach music*** continues.

Selected General Scheduling References

Canady, Robert Lynn and Michael D. Rettig. *Block Scheduling: A Catalyst for Change in High Schools*. Princeton, NJ: Eye On Education, 1995.

Canady, Robert Lynn and Michael D. Rettig, Eds. *Teaching in the Block: Strategies for Engaging Active Learners*. Larchmont, NY: Eye On Education, 1997.

Gainey, Donald D. and John M. Brucato. *Questions & Answers about Block Scheduling: An Implementation Guide*. Larchmont, NY: Eye On Education, 1999.

Keefe, James W. and John M. Jenkins. *Instruction and the Learning Environment*. Larchmont, NY: Eye On Education, 1997.

Marshak, David. *Action Research on Block Scheduling*. Larchmont, NY: Eye On Education, 1997.

Selected
Music Scheduling
References

Connors, Thomas N. "A Survey of Block Scheduling Implementation in the Florida Public Secondary Schools and Its Effect on Band Programs." Ph.D. diss., Florida State University, 1997.

Hall, Gary E. "The Effects of the Four-Period Day on Colorado High School Performing Arts Classes," Master thesis, Adams State College, 1992.

Lowther, Raymond W. Suttle. "Music Teachers' Perceptions of the Effect of Block Scheduling on Enrollment and Ensemble Balance in High School Performing Arts Classes in the Commonwealth of Virginia." Ed.D. diss., George Washington University, 1997.

Miles, Richard and Larry Blocher. *Block Scheduling: Implications for Music Education*. Springfield, IL: Focus on Excellence, 1996.

Scheduling Time for Music. Reston, VA: Music Educators National Conference, 1995.

Selected
Teaching Music
References

Ables, Hal, Charles Hoffer and Robert Klotman. *Foundations of Music Education*. Second Edition, New York: Schirmer, 1994.

American School Band Directors Association. *The New ASBDA Curriculum Guide: A Reference Book for School Band Directors*. Miami, FL: Belwin-Mills/Warner Bros., 1997.

Band Music Guide, 1996 edition. Northfield, IL: The Instrumentalist, 1996.

Battisti, Frank. *The Twentieth Century American Wind Band/Ensemble: History, Development, and Literature*. Ft. Lauderdale, FL: Meredith Music Publications, 1995.

Battisti, Frank and Robert Garofalo. *Guide to Score Study for The Wind Band Conductor*. Ft. Lauderdale, FL: Meredith Music Publications, 1990.

Brinson, Barbara A. *Choral Music: Methods and Materials*. New York: Schirmer Books, 1996.

Colwell, Richard J. *The Evaluation of Music Teaching and Learning*. Englewood Cliffs, NJ: Prentice-Hall, Inc., 1970.

Colwell, Richard J. and Thomas Goolsby. *The Teaching of Instrumental Music*. Second Edition. Englewood Cliffs, NJ: Prentice-Hall, Inc., 1992.

The Complete String Guide: Standards, Programs, Purchase, and Maintenance. Reston, VA: A joint publication of ASTA, MENC, and NSOA, 1988.

Dillon, Jacquelyn A. and Casimer B. Kriechbaum, Jr. *How to Design and Teach a Successful School String and Orchestra Program*. San Diego, CA: Neil A. Kjos, 1978.

Durante, Leonard P., *et al*. *Band Music That Works*, Volumes I and II. Burlingham, CA: Contrapuntal Publications, 1988.

Dvorak, Thomas L., Cynthia Crump Taggert and Peter Schmalz. *Best Music for Young Band*. Brooklyn, NY: Manhattan Beach Music, 1986.

Elliott, David J. *Music Matters*. New York, NY: Oxford University Press, 1995.

Ericksen, Connie M. *Band Director's Curriculum Resource*. West Nyack, NY: Parker Publishing Company, 1998.

Garofalo, Robert. *Blueprint for Band*. Ft. Lauderdale, FL: Meredith Music Publications, 1983.

Green, Elizabeth A.H. *The Dynamic Orchestra*. Englewood Cliffs, NJ: Prentice-Hall, Inc., 1987.

Haasemann, Frauke and James M. Jordan. *Group Vocal Technique*. Chapel Hill, NC: Hinshaw Music, Inc., 1991.

Haasemann, Frauke and James M. Jordan. *Group Vocal Technique: The Vocalise Cards*. Chapel Hill, NC: Hinshaw Music, Inc., 1992.

Hawaii Music Program, Curriculum Research and Development Group, College of Education, and the University of Hawaii. *Comprehensive Musicianship Through Band Performance*. Zone 4, Book A by Brent Heisenger. Menlo Park, CA: Addison-Wesley Publishing Company, 1973.

Hoffer, Charles. *Introduction to Music Education*. Belmont, CA: Wadsworth, 1983.

Hoffer, Charles. *Teaching Music in the Secondary Schools*. Fourth Edition. Belmont, CA: Wadsworth, 1991.

Jordan, James. *Evoking Sound*. Chicago, IL: GIA Publications, 1996.

Keene, James A. *A History of Music Education in the United States*. Hanover, NH: University Press of New England, 1982.

Kohut, Daniel L. *Instrumental Pedagogy: Teaching Techniques for School Band and Orchestra Directors*. Englewood Cliffs, NJ: Prentice-Hall, Inc., 1973.

Kohut, Daniel L. *Musical Performance: Learning Theory and Pedagogy*. Englewood Cliffs, NJ: Prentice-Hall, Inc., 1985.

Labuta, Joseph A. *Guide to Accountability in Music Instruction*. West Nyack, NY: Parker Publishing Co., Inc., 1974.

Labuta, Joseph A. *Teaching Musicianship in the High School Band*. Revised Edition. Ft. Lauderdale, FL: Meredith Music Publications, 1997.

Lautzenheiser, Tim. *The Art of Successful Teaching: A Blend of Content and Context*. Chicago, IL: GIA Publications, 1992.

Lautzenheiser, Tim. *The Joy of Inspired Teaching*. Chicago, IL: GIA Publications, 1993.

Lehman, Paul. *Tests and Measurements in Music*. Englewood Cliffs, NJ: Prentice-Hall, Inc., 1968.

Leonhard, Charles and Robert W. House. *Foundations and Principles of Music Education*. New York: McGraw-Hill, 1972.

Lisk, Edward S. *The Creative Director: Alternative Rehearsal Techniques*. Third Edition. Ft. Lauderdale, FL: Meredith Music Publications, 1991.

Madsen, Charles H. and Clifford K. Madsen. *Teaching and Discipline: A Positive Approach for Educational Development*. Third Edition. Raleigh, NC: Contemporary Publishing Co., 1983.

Madsen, Clifford K. and Cornelia Yarbrough. *Competency-Based Music Education*. Englewood Cliffs, NJ: Prentice-Hall, Inc., 1980.

Mayer, Frederick R., Editor. *The String Superlist*. Reston, VA: MENC, 1993.

Miles, Richard, Editor. *Teaching Music through Performance in Band*, Volumes I, II, and III. Chicago, IL: GIA Publications, 1996, 1998, 1999.

Miller, Richard. *The Structure of Singing*. New York: Schirmer Books, 1986.

National Band Association, *Selective Music List for Bands*, Third Edition. Nashville, TN: National Band Association, 1990.

Pizer, Russell A. *Instrumental Music Evaluation Kit*. West Nyack, NY: Parker Publishing Company, 1987.

Rehrig, William H. *The Heritage Encyclopedia of Band Music*, Volumes I and II. Westerville, OH: Integrity Press, 1991.

Rehrig, William H. *The Heritage Encyclopedia of Band Music*. Edited by Paul Bierley, Volume III Supplement. Westerville, OH: Integrity Press, 1996.

Reimer, Bennett. *A Philosophy of Music Education*. Second Edition. Englewood Cliffs, NJ: Prentice-Hall, Inc., 1989.

Schleuter, S.L. *A Sound Approach to Teaching Instrumentalists*. Second Edition. New York, NY: Schirmer Books, 1997.

Swanwick, Keith. *Music, Mind, and Education*. London, England: Routledge, 1988.

The University of the State of New York, The State Education Department, Bureau of Curriculum Development. *Music in the Middle/Junior High School: Syllabus/ Handbook*. Albany, NY: New York State Education Department, 1988.

Walker, D.E. *Teaching Music: Managing the Successful Program*. Second Edition. New York, NY: Schirmer Books, 1998.

Webb, Guy B., Ed. *Up Front!* Boston, MA: ECS Publishing, 1993.

Williamson, John E., Compiler. Edited by Ken Neidig. *Rehearsing the Band*. Cloudcroff, NM: Neidig Services, 1998.

Willson, David. *Starting Beginner Band Students*. Revised Edition. Springfield, IL: Focus on Excellence, 1996.

Wisconsin Department of Public Instruction. *A Guide to Curriculum Planning in Music Education*. Madison, WI: Wisconsin Department of Public Education, 1986.

About the Authors

Dr. Larry R. Blocher is Associate Professor of Music Education, Associate Director of Bands, and Director of Music Education at Wichita State University in Wichita, Kansas. At Wichita State Dr. Blocher conducts the concert band, teaches undergraduate and graduate music education courses, and coordinates the music education program. Dr. Blocher received his BME and MM (music education and performance) degrees from Morehead State University in Kentucky, and his Ph.D. in Music Education from The Florida State University. His teaching background includes university teaching as Assistant Director of Bands and Coordinator of Music Education at Morehead State University (KY), Chair of Music Education at Syracuse University (NY), and Assistant Director of Bands at the University of Dayton (OH), and public school teaching as a band director in Kentucky and Florida. Dr. Blocher is President-Elect of the Kansas Bandmasters Association, a member-at-large representative for the National Band Association, and a member of the Editorial Committee for the *Music Educators Journal* (MEJ). Dr. Blocher is active as a guest clinician/conductor/adjudicator and has presented clinic/research sessions at international, national, regional, and state conferences in the area of instrumental music teacher preparation.

Dr. Richard B. Miles is Professor of Music and Director of Bands at Morehead State University in Kentucky, holds a Doctor of Philosophy degree from The Florida State University, and undergraduate and graduate degrees from Appalachian State University and the University of Illinois. In addition to the supervision and administration of the MSU Bands, Dr. Miles teaches undergraduate and graduate conducting. Since coming to MSU in 1985, the MSU Symphony Band, under his direction, has been selected to perform for conventions of the Music Educators National Conference, College Band Directors National Association, National Band Association, and the Kentucky Music Educators Association. Dr. Miles is Past President of the College Band Directors National Association – Southern Division, and is in demand as a guest conductor, clinician, and adjudicator. Internationally, he has conducted concerts and clinics throughout Europe, The United Kingdom, Canada, and The People's Republic of China.

Dr. Blocher and Dr. Miles are authors of more than 30 articles and co-authors of *Teaching Music through Performance in Band*, Volumes I, II, and III (GIA Publications, 1996, 1998, 1999), *Block Scheduling: Implications for Music Education* and *Scheduling and Teaching Music* (Focus on Excellence, 1996, 1999), *High School Restructuring – Block Scheduling: Implications for Music Educators* (Kentucky Coalition for Music Education, 1995), and contributors to *High School Restructuring: Additional Resources* (Kentucky Coalition for Music Education, 1996).